A CATHOLIC NUN'S
STORY
CONVENT SEXUAL ABUSE

PAULINE HURTT

LifeRich
PUBLISHING

LifeRich Publishing is a registered trademark of The Reader's Digest Association, Inc.

LifeRich Publishing books may be ordered through booksellers or by contacting:

LifeRich Publishing
1663 Liberty Drive
Bloomington, IN 47403
www.liferichpublishing.com
1 (888) 238-8637

ISBN: 978-1-4897-2796-1 (sc)
ISBN: 978-1-4897-2797-8 (e)

Print information available on the last page.

LifeRich Publishing rev. date: 03/31/2020

CONTENTS

DEDICATION

I dedicate this memoir to my Dad, Vincent and my Mom,
Florence in appreciation for what they taught me.

PART I

CHAPTER 1

The Bus Ride

The first southbound bus into New York City was due to arrive at 7:00 am. The southwest corner of the five-lane major intersection had no trees. There was a 10-foot, curved, protective glass hood with a grey plastic bench and a green trash can. The sunrise had a hint of red-orange and it looked to be a warm September day.

There were only two women waiting for that bus at 6:55 am on the first Saturday after Labor Day, 1966, fifty-four years ago. The 1960s are synonymous with tumultuous history: Dr. Martin Luther King and John F. Kennedy assassinations, Woodstock, Watergate, Richard Nixon's impeachment and Vietnam.

Egalitarianism reigned. There were unusually high numbers of young people joining the Peace Corps, entering convents, and attending seminaries. This counteracted the drafting of thousands of young men to serve in the Army. All of this had social ramifications. The job market was filled with openings at all levels of finance, marketing, teaching, manufacturing, and sales.

The bus arrived, and the two women boarded, paid the fare and sat next to each other towards the back of the bus. The ride into New York City was about 30 minutes. The bus stopped at the Terminal with access to the city by buses headed north, south, and east. A major subway station led into Manhattan on the A train. Here there were at least 6 tracks for subway cars traveling North or South along the West side of New York City. It was the Columbus Circle metro rail station.

The younger of the two women headed South. The older woman headed North. It was considered early for a Saturday morning, but the subway cars were sixty percent full. One could sit alone in a jumper seat or along a long row of plastic seats on either side of the car. Above were handrails secured by poles the length of each car section. Sliding doors connected one car to the next. Retractable doors for exit and entrance were at three positions in each car on both sides.

The women who had parted in the morning reunited at the same place about 1:00 pm. Then, a subway ride North went back to the Bus Terminal where they could catch the bus heading back to Parkland County. The route was west across the Bridge to Route 9 North through New Jersey into New York State.

Parkland County was on the west side of the Hudson River near the Palisades (steep rock formations) in northeastern New Jersey. Parkland County was a booming suburb of New York City connected now to Westchester County by the Tappan Zee built in the late 1960s and rebuilt in 2018. The length of the bridge span is the longest across the Hudson River.

The two women lived in the same house. They were both teachers in the local K-8 school. The younger one was returning from a graduate Geology class. The other woman was returning from a graduate Reading Methods class. There was a hint of Fall in the air. The leaves on the maple trees had started to lose their green color. Orange, yellow and red leaves were emerging as the hours of sunlight continued to diminish.

CHAPTER 2

The Early Years

Pauline was walking home with her four-year-old brother from a nearby park called "The Oval" – named such because of its shape. Its other name was The Reservoir. In the late 1800s, it had been an actual reservoir carrying water from the Catskill Mountains to the North Bronx. There were two levels in the park. The upper oval was lined with trees and park benches with concrete bases and wooden slat seats with similar back rests. A ramp led down to the lower level. There were fenced baseball diamonds to the right with a group of school-age boys playing stick ball. To the left was an asphalt black top with numerous wooden swings hung with chain ropes. The chains were long enough to allow very high swings, almost perpendicular to the top horizontal pipe - such scary fun.

An oval clay track was in the center of this lower level surrounded by tennis courts, bike paths, all fenced areas. There were see-saws and monkey bars near the front entrance to the park on this lower level. In the center of the track was a beautiful green grassy area. Pauline tossed a ball to her brother in the grass because he had tired of the toddler swings very quickly. After 30 minutes, the walk back home was four city blocks: first, North on Perry Avenue, then East down 209th Street past Hull Avenue and Decatur Avenue to the corner of Parkside Place. On the corner was a square, red brick building of five stories where Pauline lived with her parents and three brothers.

The apartment "house" was one of four buildings on East 209th Street between Decatur Avenue and Parkside Place. The bricks were a dark red color with an entranceway of three grey stone steps called the "stoop". Five adults could sit squeezing onto the top step; toddlers could sit on the bottom step. Spring, summer, and fall you would find one of your neighbors leaning into the corner on the top step.

Across the street another red brick five story building faced the stoop. There was a woman in one of those apartments who sat at her kitchen window facing the street despite the weather. She especially liked the evenings; she sat by the open window leaning her body out the windowsill. Pauline noticed her at all times of the day just looking up the hill and glaring at anyone walking home.

All the apartment buildings had horizontal iron "fire escapes" connected vertically by rungs from 2 fifth floor windows, down to the fourth-floor windows, to the third-floor windows and lastly, the second-floor windows. The first floor was only 10 feet from the ground. The fire escapes could be seen on all of the four sides of the building. The renters used those iron slats to hold plants and/or to dry a towel or two.

A seventh grader, Pauline was 12 years old in 1954. She was the firstborn child of four belonging to Florence and Vincent. Vincent was a professional musician and marketing manager for CBS recordings. Florence had been a buyer for a famous New York City department store. She was now a creative homemaker making ends meet from week to week. The delivery of her four children had been difficult and fraught with uncertainty and angst.

The second child was born in the hallway of the apartment building on the third floor. Vincent was with his wife when Florence collapsed on the floor of the hallway with the baby's head protruding. The baby boy was healthy. The bleeding was profuse and within forty-eight hours she developed a high fever. She had contracted child-birth fever because of the lack of sterile instruments. Vincent had no time to wash his hands as he delivered his son. Florence was seriously ill in the double bed in the only bedroom in the three-room apartment. The family physician, Dr. Mc Norris, made another house call three days after the birth. He told Florence and Vincent he was going to administer an injection of a new drug. He did not know if it would help. Little was known about penicillin in 1944. It was first used during World War II after amputations and lacerations. It had been effective in those situations preventing bacterial infections.

Florence's mother, Bertha, a slight woman with a stern demeanor, was there to take care of the baby, John, and Pauline. The bottles had to be sterilized and only warm pasteurized milk given to the baby. Pauline was not eating because at 22 months she sat and cried asking for her mother over and over. She was inconsolable and Bertha knew only one way to get a child to cooperate. That was with a good spanking with her pants pulled down. You can imagine the effect that first spanking had on Pauline.

Then, after seven days, with an injection of penicillin every day, Florence's fever broke! It was Saturday, Bertha was gone, Vincent took Pauline's hand and went to the bedroom door. He opened it eight inches. Finally, the child saw her mother. Florence patted her head and told her to be a good girl while she stayed in bed too weak to yet get out of bed. In later years, as a young adult, she put this story together from information told her by her dear Aunt Betty and Bertha, her grandmother.

The third birth 6 years later was fraught with worry about getting to the hospital on time. Florence did not want another home birth. There were two false alarms; Vincent drove as fast as he could to the hospital ten miles away. Pauline was 8 years-old and her brother, John, was 6 years-old. One morning Florence's water broke. She frantically called her husband to get home. Instead, Vincent's father, Harry, showed up in a taxicab and took Florence to the hospital. The woman was in tears. Accidentally, Pauline and John were left alone for the entire day to fend for themselves. When Vincent finally came home late that evening, he told them they had a new baby brother. Florence had named him Gerard in honor of St. Gerard, patron Saint of expecting mothers. The two siblings had never heard of such a name. They questioned their Dad about such an obscure name.

The newborn, Gerard, was in his bassinette when Pauline and John came home from school for lunch a week after the birth. They were astounded because this baby had a head full of black hair. What a shock to them. Pauline kept asking, first her mother and

7

next her father, "How could a new-born have a full head of hair?" Their answer was they did not know.

Three years later, in 1953, Florence was pregnant again at age 39. In her eighth month she knew the birth was going to be a breach birth. One more thing for her to worry about. Pauline was 11 years-old and John was 9 years-old. Taking care of the two year-old, Gerard, was Pauline's responsibility The breach birth carried specific dangers because the umbilical cord could be wrapped around the neck of the newborn and cause a loss of oxygen to the brain. In late April the family had another boy, Tyler, who weighed less than his siblings at birth. He looked very small in the bassinette on his first day home.

As a matter of fact, at 6 months of age, Tyler developed pneumonia and was hospitalized in a place where there was an infant ward. Florence had to take three buses to get to the hospital to see her baby lying in a crib with a fever and a cough. After 7 days in the hospital, Tyler's lungs were clear. The doctor told Florence that the boy would probably be suspect to lung infections all his life. The burden of care for her two brothers at this time fell once again on the shoulders of Pauline. She fed them in the evening – Tyler with a bottle and Gerard, now 3 years old, with mashed food. Most of that food he did not like. It was a challenge for Pauline to get the baby spoon in Gerard's mouth. All of these stories Pauline remembered into her old age.

CHAPTER 3

Sister Zachariah

Both of her parents had high expectations of Pauline. She was a serious student popular among her peers. There was a group of her friends who all lived in other apartment buildings on the same street, East 209th. They attended the neighborhood Catholic school staffed by nuns. These particular nuns wore habits and stiff black veils on top of their white covered heads. All one could see were eyebrows, eyes, a nose, and a dour mouth.

Pauline took piano lessons every week. The lessons started when she was five years old at the wishes of her musician father. Fear and nervousness plagued her at the Spring piano recitals. Pauline was not very self-confident. There was an old ebony upright piano in the apartment that was tuned every year by the portly piano man, Mr. Ed. It was an ugly piece of furniture against gray painted walls. Pauline had to practice new music pieces after school every day. Vincent came to realize that his daughter did not have the natural ability that he possessed. Vincent was able to play a song by just listening to the melody. As they say, he "played by ear". Pauline continued with piano lessons as well as practicing for ten more years. The greatest benefit of all those lessons was Pauline's ability to read music and play simple tunes for the rest of her life.

In October, the young girls in the seventh grade were recruited to help in the sacristy of the Church affiliated with the school. The sacristy is the room behind the altar and sanctuary. The altar is where a priest says Mass. Pauline and her friends volunteered. They would spend 30 minutes of their lunch hour "working" in the sacristy. They would gather and chat as adolescents do. Dusting the furniture and sweeping the floor took all of five minutes. The nun in charge of the sacristy and all of its contents was Sister Zachariah, a young, new nun who taught second graders.

Sister Zachariah, tall and thin with long, black rosary beads hanging off her black belt, became a hero of sorts to Pauline. Normally there was no outside contact with the nun in the classroom. This situation was different. There were conversations with Sister Zachariah about the weather, the basketball game, and the tests on Friday. Sister Zachariah always asked her these questions. Pauline had found a substitute for the one-on-one attention she did not get from her parents. Very slowly she was developing a liking for Sister Zachariah. She looked forward to lunchtime every day and enjoyed talking with her new idol.

Back at home, as the eldest of her siblings, three brothers, Pauline reacted to the pressure of responsibility very willingly. She was in charge of dinner and bedtime for the two youngest – the four-year old and the infant. Seventh grade homework was not a challenge, just busy work. That left her with time for chores, such as washing the dishes and drying them and putting them all away. The oldest brother, John, was in fifth grade. He had a paper route that kept him away from the chores associated with dinnertime.

That same sense of responsibility spilled over to the sacristy job. She was a keen observer and learned exactly what to do with the clothes, called vestments, that the priests wore for daily Mass. The chasuble, the stole, the amice, and the alb became new vocabulary words for Pauline. There were wide horizontal drawers about three inches deep to store the different colors of the vestments lying flat in the drawer. Some were everyday vestments and others were special occasion vestments. She kept the drawers very tidy and organized. It didn't take long for her to learn the way the vestments were laid out for the priests, who lived in the rectory - a two-story home adjacent to the Church.

Another task in the Church that took a lot of time was cleaning the brass candelabras that held five candles placed on either side of the altar. At the base of each candle was a round, clear glass dish that filled with the melted dripping wax. Pauline and her friends cleaned those little glass dishes on Fridays. One side of the sacristy on the lower level was for the altar boys who wore cassocks and surplices. Some of these clothes were always thrown on the floor and the girls had to hang them up.

A couple of the girls dropped out of the sacristy volunteer job by the time they reached eighth grade. There were new seventh graders that needed to be trained. Pauline was given that responsibility. Conversations with Sister Zachariah continued every day throughout the second year. By this second year Pauline became curious about the woman behind the veil. Where did she grow up? What was her real name? Did she have brothers and sisters? Eventually Pauline actually received answers to *all* those questions. What a violation of boundaries! Sister Zachariah perhaps had no idea of the relationship she was forging with this impressionable teenager – or did she?

CHAPTER 4

High School

Pauline graduated from that neighborhood Catholic elementary school in June of 1955 at the age of thirteen. Into her later years, she still remembered that first day of high school in September of the same year. It was a traumatic day for her. All of Pauline's friends from the neighborhood were attending the local high school staffed by the nuns of the same order (community) as the elementary school. She remembers that two-mile walk from her home all the way down Decatur Avenue. It stopped at Moshula Parkway; on the other side of this four-lane parkway she went through different neighborhoods. Her walk ended at the all-girls high school that sat on top of a steep hill. Her friends referred to it as Snob Hill.

Thanks to her father who insisted she take the Entrance Exam and then attend this privileged high school, she walked alone into a foreign building with 70 other young freshman girls. The course of study was rigorous - Algebra, Latin, English, History, and Science. She tried out for the basketball team and was selected to play. She also chose the Glee Club as an extra-curricular activity. Between the glee club practices and the basketball practices and games, she was no longer available to her mother for caring for her two young brothers after school. She rarely got home before 5 pm. She still had to take care of the baby, Tyler, at feeding time and bedtime.

She was thrust into a new life that excluded Sister Zachariah who had been assigned to a school in upstate New York. That was a loss for the teenager overshadowed by the start of the school year in September. Pauline faithfully wrote weekly letters to Sister Zachariah. Return mail was not forthcoming so she finally stopped writing to her except on holidays.

The distractions of a large amount of homework kept her mind occupied. During the Christmas vacation, Sister Zachariah returned to New York City to visit with her family. She invited Pauline to visit her at 7 pm one evening at a different convent located in Queens. Her mother did not want to see the thirteen-year-old travelling the subways alone in the dark on those winter nights. She forbade her from going to see Sister Zachariah. That was a crushing blow to Pauline. She so yearned to see the adult who had paid attention to what she had to say. She missed her terribly and sulked for two or three days.

Back at school after Christmas, quite unexpectedly, Pauline was voted Class President of her Homeroom. She had never before been singled out for an honor like this one. She walked home that day with her head held high. Pauline had become somebody – a member of the Student Council as President of her class. Slowly she had developed new friends. Unfortunately, they did not live in her neighborhood. Those new friends were bus rides away from her.

Some Saturday nights they would gather at one friend's house for a party. The bus rides home after 10 pm were scary for the anxious teenager. Her curfew was 11 pm.

One morning during Homeroom in her Junior year, Pauline was paged down to the Treasurer's Office. Her father's check for $20.00, her monthly tuition, had bounced. The nun told her not to fall behind on her payments. That was the first clue Pauline had that things were not all right with her Dad. Sure enough, during her Junior year at the same high school, Vincent moved out of the house. Money was in short supply for rent, food, clothes and bus fares.

By this time, Pauline had a Saturday job in Manhattan in the Credit Department of a large Fifth Avenue department store. It was basically a simple filing job. She got a biweekly paycheck that she turned over to her mother. That part-time job became a summer job for Pauline. Riding the subways on 90-degree days was extremely uncomfortable. This was not the age of air conditioners.

Prior to her Dad leaving his wife and four children, Pauline was making all the beds one morning when she found an empty medium-sized liquor bottle under his pillow. She later found the vanilla bottle in the kitchen cabinet empty when she began baking a cake. She didn't know the word "alcoholic" until she was an adult, however, that was the fate of her Dad at age 44. By her Senior year at the High School he lost his job for embezzlement. It had become a very anxious time for this seventeen-year old who had to assume more and more responsibility at home caring for her three brothers. Her mother had found a part-time job in the neighborhood. Pauline never found out who was paying the rent on their apartment as well as her tuition at the high school. Perhaps it was her grandfather who knew the value of the education she was getting at Snob Hill. Later on, as an adult, this seemed very plausible.

It was on the day of her graduation from high school, June 19th, 1959, that her father was hospitalized for internal bleeding. Graduation day was not a happy one for her. As a matter of fact, Pauline was the only one to visit her father in the hospital every day after graduation. That visit meant taking three city buses to get to the far away City Hospital for indigents. To this day she does not understand why her mother never went to visit him. The last time Pauline was with him before a coma settled over his body, her Dad asked her to recite the Rosary prayers with him. So, Pauline sat on a chair pulled close to the bed next to his shoulder. Her Dad was alive in an "oxygen tent" built up and around his bed out of cloudy heavy plastic sheets.

Because the rosary prayers are so repetitious, Pauline said them aloud by rote, with little thought. At the start of the second decade of ten Hail Mary prayers, her father raised his voice and said, "Can't you say the prayers slowly?" She was so surprised at his voice that she continued at a snail's pace until the five decades of Hail Mary's were finished. Little did she realize that this was last time she would speak to her father alive. Vincent slipped into a coma that night. He passed away early on a Sunday morning in late July of sclerosis of the liver – one month after her graduation from high school.

What Pauline remembered for her whole life was the sight of a hospital doctor in a white coat sitting in the living room. Vincent's father, Harry, called Florence to tell her he absolutely did not want an autopsy performed on his son. Florence, always a narcissist, signed those autopsy papers in spite of Pauline's protests. She was witness to her mother's signature. Florence seemed to have no respect or gratitude for Harry who was paying all of his son's bills including his four grandchildren's bills.

None of her three brothers were home that summer. John was a camp counselor about an hour away from his Bronx home. Gerard and Tyler were living with an aunt and uncle at their summer home in the central Pennsylvania mountains. Only John was notified of his Dad's death early on that Sunday morning. He came home Monday morning visibly in shock that his father had died. He was so distraught that he had not had a chance to see his Dad alive for the last time. John was close to Vincent. He constantly received praise from his father for almost everything he did.

Enter Sister Zachariah who had contacted Pauline again. She had heard of her father's death. She planned a visit. Pauline had not lost her affection for this nun from the sacristy of old. Sister Zachariah gave her a gift - black rosary beads. They discussed whether or not she had a "vocation", i.e. a calling to serve God as a nun.

After high school *all* of her friends were attending College. She accepted a full-time job with a corporation in lower Manhattan near Wall Street. Pauline agreed to take the job to support her family for *one* year only. Before she took the job, she had made up her mind to enter the convent and become a nun just like Sister Zachariah. Four years in high school had not taught her anything about real life in the world. Dating was not in her equation that year. She was adamant about her decision. Her Protestant aunts and uncles were furious with her mother. They blamed Florence, a Catholic convert, for Pauline's involvement with the Catholic Church.

In the Spring of 1960, Pauline hitched a ride with a classmate. They drove to Parkland County to the Headquarters of the community of nuns where the Superior (Mother General) resided. She petitioned this person, the Mother General, for entry into the convent. Of course, she was accepted! Did Sister Zachariah realize the effect she had had on this young woman?

PART II

CHAPTER 5

Entrance Day

Se, 1960, dawned clear, cool, and sunny. It was Entrance Day for Pauline. Around 1:00 pm she was on the grounds of the Motherhouse standing on the grass outside the new two-story Novitiate building. Her two best friends from high school, Anne and Carolyn, were with her. Of course, her mother and two youngest brothers, ages 7 and 10, were there, as well as her dear Aunt Betty and her two grandmothers. Someone took pictures for the last time of Pauline dressed in secular clothes and shoes. In a small black suitcase was her new black postulant dress and veil, white underwear, a black belt, black stockings and shoes. She also had the black rosary beads that Sister Zachariah had given her the prior year.

At 2:00 pm, the 60 new postulants entered the Novitiate building. The nun in charge was Sister Frances, the Postulant Mistress. She assigned beds to the young women in the order of their "rank". Rank was based on the order they had petitioned the Mother

General in the Spring. Pauline was in the middle somewhere. This first floor had five open dormitories that contained ten beds with hospital-like curtains around each bed. There was a closet, attached to three drawers, and a straight back chair. That was it. Pauline's new abode. The large bathroom with five stalls, five showers and five sinks was at the rear of the first-floor dormitories. There was a list of shower times for each dorm – 10 minutes/dorm for ten people.

After all the new postulants had changed into their black garb, they carried the suitcase back out to their families and said good-bye to them. This was it. The day Pauline had dreamed about was beginning.

A tour of the Novitiate building included a large Community Room with eight 8-foot rectangular tables and chairs. It was at the opposite end of the first-floor dormitories. Up to the second floor, where the 2nd year Novices lived, they visited the small chapel. On the lower level, the basement of the building, was a huge laundry room, two trunk rooms, a coat room, and finally the recreation room with hard-back chairs. There was a piano in the room and small square tables. What is a "trunk" room? Each postulant had a large black cargo trunk that they shipped to the Novitiate before Entrance Day. In the trunk were things such as a robe, new underwear, another pair of shoes, stockings, toiletries such as soap, shampoo, and personal hygiene, sheets, notebooks, prayer books, missals, umbrella, boots, and a black coat. Pauline had also included as part of her belongings the piano sheet music that she liked to use.

In the laundry room on the far wall were open cubicles labelled with their names. In the days to come, their clean sheets and clean underwear, washed by a Novice (a 2nd year aspirant) in charge of the laundry, would be tossed into their bin. Every item of clothing had fabric name tapes sewn into them. The room even had a mangle - two long, large 12-inch round heated rollers touching each other. They moved simultaneously in opposite directions. The mangle pressed the nuns' habits (clothes). It also dried and pressed the sheets and pillowcases. The postulants never washed their one black dress. Only their undershirt was washed daily.

By 4:00 pm it was time to assemble in the coat room to prepare to walk over to the Motherhouse, the main convent building. The large chapel looked more like a cathedral.

The path from the Novitiate over to the main building was narrow and ¾ of a mile long. They were told to walk in pairs, in order of rank, and recite the rosary prayers together. At 5:00 pm they were in this large chapel for Vespers. Vespers were psalms that were chanted in Latin by all the nuns including the Novices. The postulants were assigned seats, called stalls, in order of rank again. Their (choir) stalls were in the very front of the chapel adjacent to the altar rail and facing each other from the left side to the right side. Pauline's stall was in the second row on the left. There was a rack for the psalm book (Office Book), a missal, a spiritual book and a retractable kneeler. That book could be a biography of a Saint or other instructional devotion book.

The nuns at this Motherhouse convent included old retired nuns, middle-aged nuns who worked there or taught at the college, and finally young, new nuns. The younger nuns were in charge of the abandoned or court-ordered young boys who lived in groups in the very old section of the main convent. In the earlier part of the 20th century this had been an orphanage for boys from New York City.

After Vespers and singing of hymns, the postulants filed out of the very large chapel through a covered walkway to the main building. These newbies were not allowed in the main dining room, called a refectory. They went downstairs to the oldest part of the Motherhouse that belonged to the young boys. The postulant refectory was a narrow, long rectangular room with seats for the sixty of them. Chairs were on both sides of two long tables with a horizontal table connecting them on the far end. This is where Sister Frances sat with two rotating postulants on either side of her chair. The meal was family style with serving dishes passed down the table. Pauline liked the hot dogs on a bun but did not care for the sauerkraut. They were told to eat what was served. The dessert that first night was a paper Dixie cup of ice cream without coffee or tea. A medium-sized plastic rectangular container with hot water and soap was delivered to the tables for every six postulants. They were instructed to wash their dishes and dry them with the towel delivered. This was not what Pauline expected. However, she was so conditioned to following orders dictated by her mother at home, that she continued following directions and doing exactly what she was told. She questioned *nothing*. However, in hindsight, what an unsanitary way to clean so many dishes and silverware!

As they filed out of the refectory single file, they were told to assemble in a line of twos in the order of rank. They proceeded back down the alley toward the main building. Eventually, the Novices told one of them that the alley was referred to as "rat alley". It was made of concrete and cement. It was also dark and damp.

Back to the main chapel for 7 pm Matins, closing psalms for the day chanted again in Latin. This time Pauline noticed the nuns on the right side chanted four lines and the left side responded with the next four lines. Back and forth the chanting in Latin went for 30 minutes. Then there was a closing hymn. The postulants were the last to file out of the chapel once more. These young women would come to spend almost five hours a day in the chapel. They walked the "Rosary" path again back to the Novitiate. There they filed into the recreation room and met the 48 Novices. Each postulant was assigned to a "Novice mother". Pauline's Novice mother was Sister Sarah. The novices had the responsibility of answering any questions the new postulant might have.

As fate would have it, Sister Sarah was somebody Pauline knew. She had been in the choir at a Church where her father was the Organist and choir director. Pauline accompanied her father every Sunday and Holy Day to that Church, south of the north Bronx where she lived. That is where her father worked part-time. There she had met two high school twins, Sadie and Joan, who were part of this parish's choir. Sister Sarah had a serious personality and obeyed all the rules to the letter. Pauline had an excellent role model. Her Novice mother was even in charge of the laundry room – a job of serious responsibility for the Novitiate.

By 9:00 pm everyone walked upstairs to get ready for bed. Lights were out at 9:30 pm and "profound silence" began until the next morning after prayers. Pauline was exhausted. No wonder, with all the adrenaline produced on this auspicious Entrance Day. She fell asleep quickly.

CHAPTER 6

Postulants

Pauline woke up to the sound of a very loud clanging that emanated from a large old-fashioned school bell. It was 5:00 am and dark outside. She got dressed before going back to the communal bathroom. There, she brushed her teeth, used the toilet, and washed her hands. Bed making was simple. By 5:30 am both the novices and postulants were ready to walk the Rosary path again for morning prayers called Lauds.

At 6 am, they gathered in the main chapel. The chanting of the psalms lasted for thirty minutes. Thirty minutes of meditation followed. The postulants did not have any lessons or guidance in meditation. It was a long 30 minutes for them before the celebration of the Mass by an appointed priest. He resided on the grounds of the convent in a small rectory.

After Mass ended, breakfast was served in the small refectory. During breakfast, a Novice read aloud a biography of St. Theresa for twenty minutes. The postulants followed the same routine after the meal. They walked back to the Novitiate in twos reciting the Rosary. All the postulants met in the Community Room sitting in assigned seats at the long tables. Sister Frances sat at the front of the room at a desk. She explained that every morning after breakfast there were chores to be done. The list of work and assignments was a long one. She called the name of the postulant and read the random assignment. Pauline was told to report to Sister Gregory at the relatively new college building adjacent to the Novitiate.

Other assignments included: the sewing room, the kitchen, the sacristy, the main convent large laundry room, the switchboard, the main refectory, the bathrooms in the Novitiate. Usually there were two or more postulants given the same assignment. Six went to the Sewing room, 3 went to the college building, 4 went to the main refectory. The work was to start the following morning right after breakfast.

Then, Sister Frances explained they were to go over to the college to assemble in a classroom. The postulants would take an Aptitude test to determine their course of study while attending the affiliated college. That test was relatively easy for Pauline because of her rigorous high school curriculum. Her four years of Latin studies made the vocabulary section easy. Her Math studies, including pre-calculus, made the math section easy. Her logic course made the analogies section easy also.

By the time testing was over, it was 11 am. Sister Frances instructed them to take a bathroom break in the Novitiate and assemble in the coat room at 11:30 am. It was time to walk the Rosary path again and back to the chapel for noon prayers. This time all of the nuns recited the rosary prayers out loud in cadence.

The main meal in their refectory followed. Today, their first full day, the postulants were given a social hour outside in a small fenced park on the grounds near the cemetery. The cemetery was on a sloping hill at the limits of the property.

Pauline approached the largest circle of postulants. She was on the outskirts of this clique as an observer. She felt isolated. The postulants in the circle seemed to know each other. She came to find out they all went to the same high school. The leader of the group was obvious. She had a strong vociferous demeanor. Matilda was very articulate. She seemed more mature than the others. Pauline was left talking with two other postulants who had attended the same elementary school as she did. Pauline was dejected. This was not as it had been at her high school where she was accepted and recognized as a leader. What an unhappy turn of events for her. Finding her place in this group of 60 proved daunting.

On the second day after breakfast, Pauline walked with two other postulants, Gabrielle and Deanna, over to the college building. There they reported to Sister Gregory, the Dean of the College. She was very happy to see the new postulants. Sister Gregory gave the three of them a grand tour. As they were walking, she talked about what they were to do every day. Dry mop the floors in the hallways and the classrooms, empty all the trash bins, and clean the bathrooms in the building until they were shining.

The large Library was off limits. There was another postulant responsible for that alone. There was also a staircase that needed to be swept every day. Downstairs near the back door was the closet with all the cleaning supplies. Sister Gregory asked if they knew how to use a large floor buffer. The buffing needed to be done on Mondays by one of them. Then, she abruptly left the three postulants to themselves. They talked, introducing themselves to each other. Deanna had come all the way from St. Louis, MO. Gabrielle was tall and thin with red hair sticking out of her postulant veil. She was very soft-spoken. Pauline immediately spoke about dividing the work equally for a week and then rotating the tasks the following week. This would be easy. No one particularly liked cleaning bathrooms so thoroughly all of the time.

Sister Frances had given directions to work until 9:30 am and then report back to the Novitiate. There they met in the community room again and sat in their assigned seats. At 10:00 am, Sister Frances gave each of them their college class schedule. Pauline did not understand why her schedule did not match the postulants sitting on either side of her. She would later discover that the Dean had put her in a "Science track" with two other postulants, Mary and Amy. Once again Pauline felt isolated. She was placed in a General Biology course at the time her peers were elsewhere. She was also missing out on a Gym class worth 2 credits.

Most of the postulants, including Pauline, were in an English Composition course followed by a Western Civilizations course. Each class was two hours in length. English in the morning and Western Civ in the afternoon. The General Biology course met on Saturday morning for three hours followed by a Lab. Pauline sat in the back row at a Lab table. The course was filled with older professed nuns with black veils. These nuns had already taken their vows of obedience, poverty, and chastity. Postulants were not allowed to speak to professed nuns. She felt very alone.

On the day Sister Jean was explaining the reproductive system with charts of female genitalia and then male genitalia, including an egg and a sperm uniting to form a fetus, Pauline's jaw dropped. She never knew how a baby was formed. In high school she had been afraid that kissing a boy would get her pregnant. Her mother had never told her about the birds and bees or sex. That was the norm for the early 50s. What a rude awakening for the young postulant. She was shocked sitting in this Lab contemplating what reproduction might feel like.

The postulants' first visit with their families occurred in October at an outdoor Fall Festival. This country Fair generated income for the main convent. There were booths with games for children, booths with handmade knitted hats and mittens for sale, tables with raffle items, and food vendors. It was a typical fall day, cool and sunny. Pauline and the other postulants spent the afternoon outside on the grounds of the Fair walking around with their families. Her mother with her two youngest boys had travelled by subway to the GWB bus terminal to catch a bus to Parkland County. It had been a two-hour journey to reach these convent grounds. The trip was not in vain. Pauline seemed happy and well fed. The four hours passed very quickly. The postulants needed to be back in the chapel before 5 pm Vespers. Good-byes felt sad and lonely to Pauline. She missed interacting with her brothers. She would not see them again until Christmas.

Since most of the postulants were 18 or 19 years old and living in close quarters following strict rules, various pranks and jokes became the norm. Sister Vincent did not know how one or two of them could sneak into the dormitories and short sheet a bed in each of the five alcoves. Of course, it was pitch dark when the victims could not get into bed. Laughter ensued after the 9:30 pm profound silence bell had rung, and lights went out. Sister Frances appeared with a flashlight, still dressed in her habit and announced it was time to stop giggling and talking. For the rest of the week Sister Frances paraded up and down the five dormitories at 9:30 pm to look for violators of the 9:30 pm bell.

Another prank occurred one morning at 5:00am. One or two postulants would find out that they could not open the curtain around their bed. Someone, very cleverly, had actually sewn the curtain closed in the dark the night before. Sounds of voices at this early time of the day usually brought Sister Lucia, the Novice Mistress, into the dorms. She simply announced, "Whoever is responsible for this prank see me after breakfast on the second floor." The punishment was usually a silent tour of duty in the kitchen peeling hundreds of potatoes or carrots.

On other occasions, one or two postulants decided they wanted to wash the only black dress they wore day in and day out. So, back to the little sinks in the lavatory they saturated the tops of the dresses with soap and water. The wet dresses were then hung on hangars over the one heater vent on the wall in the dorm. Now, because the heat was turned down after 10 pm, the dresses did not fully dry. Can you imagine walking over the Rosary path in 10-degree frigid weather with a cold wet dress that filtered through to their long sleeve undershirt? Those postulants were shivering by the time they got to the main chapel. They suffered for hours on those winter days.

Undoubtedly the worst prank of all was to have your three drawers of underwear and socks and personal items taken! They only returned sometime the next day. A prank like this was blamed on one of the 2nd year Novices. The culprit was never discovered all through the long winter months.

Another failed attempt to let the night spring air breeze through the one-piece black postulant dress happened when Monica hung her dress out the open window on a wire hangar that she secured with a black sock. In the morning, you can guess what happened – the dress had fallen off the hangar and was two stories down lying in the wet dewy grass. How discouraging was that?

Thus, did the postulancy continue for nine months. The daily schedule did not vary much through the winter months. Pauline was often very cold walking that Rosary path, back and forth, three or four times a day. The March sunshine came; it slowly melted all the snow, and daffodils peeked through the ground. The Rosary path was lined with white and pink dogwood trees. When they bloomed at the beginning of May, it signaled the next great event for these seasoned postulants. It was called Reception Day.

CHAPTER 7

Reception Day

Reception Day for the 52 postulants (8 of them decided they did not have a vocation) was May 8th, 1961. This day was significant because it was a ceremony that presented the young women as brides of Jesus Christ. They would receive the religious name they had chosen, as well as the habit (clothes) of these particular nuns. The only difference was they would wear white veils instead of black veils for a year.

Pauline had chosen the name Sister Vincent in honor of her father. Deanna chose Sister Herman and Gabrielle chose Sister Alexander. When they knelt at the altar rail dressed in very old, ugly, used bridal gowns, they were individually given their name and the pieces of their muslin habit. At that time, they retreated behind the sanctuary to the sacristy to greet the nun who had sponsored them. Pauline was so very excited. She would finally see Sister Zachariah again. What a special day to get dressed in the robes of this religious community. Sister Vincent would finally look like her idol, Sister Zachariah. To her dismay she did not see the tall nun as she had anticipated. A stranger approached her. Her name was Sister Wilomena, Sister Zachariah's sponsor. Sister Vincent fought back tears. How could this be - a stranger with a cheerful face to help her get dressed for the first time in her very own habit. Sister Wilomena said something about Sister Zachariah being too far away in upstate New York to make the trip to this main convent in Parkland County.

Once again, a terrible turn of events for Sister Vincent. After the two-hour ceremony ended, the new novices, with hands hidden under their scapulars (the long narrow garment over their robes), walked outside the chapel to meet with their families – yet another auspicious day. Still feeling disappointed at not seeing Sister Zachariah, Sister Vincent found her mother, two younger brothers, her favorite aunt and two grandmothers. The lake, adjacent to the chapel grounds, was abloom with pink magnolia trees and budding maple trees. The afternoon was sunny and breezy with clear blue skies. The visit abounded with photographs and congratulations. This was the reward of the postulancy. They were Novices now.

A year of intense religious study with little to no contact with the outside world ensued. They did not attend college classes for the year. They did not see their families except in October again at the Fall Festival. Her novice guide, Sister Sarah, had moved out of the Novitiate. She was a professed nun with a black veil now. Sister Vincent had no idea where she was. The first morning they finally ate breakfast in the main refectory. They sat at two long tables with tablecloths and cloth napkins at the back of the refectory's long narrow room. Afterwards, they met in the Novitiate. Now they lived on the second floor with the same arrangement of five dormitories with ten beds each. Their community room was directly above the room they had used last year.

Sister Lucia, with a ruddy complexion and a stern demeanor, was the Novice Mistress. She rarely smiled. Her voice, however, was kind and compassionate. She explained to her new class of novices that their work assignments would occupy all of the morning. She had posted a list of those workplaces. Then she explained the serving of food in the refectory. That task involved six novices for every meal. They needed to learn how to pour coffee very slowly and bring steaming water to the tables for tea. Another two novices were responsible for washing all the pots and pans from the kitchen. The servers removed dishes from the tables and brought them into the kitchen's dishwasher. Then there would be a second meal for those servers and pot washers. Other novices drew that assignment to serve the second breakfast, dinner, and supper.

Sister Vincent's work assignment was the Novitiate laundry room all by herself. Once again, she felt isolated. She was there in the Novitiate building alone every morning. There were two washing machines and two dryers. Next to the supporting beam in the middle of the room was a long table for folding all the underwear she washed every single day. For some reason this job entailed other responsibilities. She had to empty trash cans from the first and second floors and take all the trash to an outside metal drum and burn the trash. Sister Vincent did not like windy days. The flames could leap to the grass and burn the field behind the building. She proceeded to learn how to fold shirts efficiently and then carry the clean underwear over to the bins and put each person's clothing in the correct bin.

She mopped the tile floor every morning and kept the room free of clutter. Sister Lucia regularly gave Sister Vincent additional tasks. The Novice Mistress liked to wash her own habit right there in the Novitiate. Sister Lucia taught Sister Vincent how to use the mangle to dry and press the habit parts. The mangle, as explained, was two long large rollers. One moved clockwise and the second counterclockwise. They were hot enough to change the water in the cloth to steam. In Sister Vincent's mind it was a job of great responsibility. She was also responsible for cleaning the Infirmary – a small room next to Sister Frances's room on the first floor. It contained a very small kitchen area and two beds.

The Novices met every afternoon in the Community Room for a lesson in the history of this particular congregation of nuns – how it started, where it started, when it started, and who started it. Those lessons were followed by instructions about each of the vows – poverty, chastity, and obedience. Poverty meant they were to hold no money in their possession. They must ask their Superior for money when needed. Money donated to them by their families must be turned over to the Superior nun, in charge of each convent. Chastity meant they were to be celibate. It also meant there were to be no particular friendships with another nun to the exclusion of others. Obedience meant they were to follow the directions and orders from the Mother General and the local Superior. Sister Vincent took all of the information with a grain of salt. She intended to honor her decision to be a Catholic nun.

Sometime during that summer of '61, Sister Vincent received

a small box wrapped in brown paper from a grocery bag. Her name and address were written in her youngest brother, Tyler's, handwriting. He was only 8 years old and was taking a gardening class at the Botanical Gardens on 250 acres of land in the Bronx. It had been designated and built as a Conservatory in 1890s. It was a two-mile walk from the apartment on East 209th Street through the Parkway across the railroad trestle bridge. Tyler trudged this distance every morning for the summer with his best friend, Willy.

Sister Vincent opened this package with great curiosity. Inside the box wrapped in three Kleenex tissues were two cherry tomatoes. They had survived the heat of the US Postal trucks. Sister Vincent had tears in her eyes. She had received his first harvest. Many years later, she was to find out that she had been a surrogate mother to Tyler from the age of 1 'til 6, when she left home to enter the "nunnery". He had felt abandoned by his older two siblings. John had also left home entering a Seminary to become a priest.

The summer passed, and it was September. The new postulants arrived September 8th. Sister Lucia told the Novices that they were to be role models for the new young women just entering the convent. That evening Sister Vincent sat with her assigned postulant, Anne. She asked questions about where the postulant had come from, who sponsored her, why she had entered the convent, and all about her family. The postulant, Anne, asked about her trunk, asked about the dungeon where they ate their meals, and what it was like to live in a dormitory. Sister Vincent liked this eighteen-year old. The two of them would get along just fine.

In the laundry, Sister Vincent's workload had just doubled. It took her much longer to wash all the underwear and dry the shirts and briefs. The folding seemed to take forever. The trash also doubled and what Sister Vincent feared the most came true. When they returned from dinner one afternoon, the fire engines were there. The grass in the field had caught fire from the burning trash or maybe the explosion of an aerosol can. Sister Vincent's heart was pounding, her palms were sweaty, and she was frozen to the spot of the fire. She was responsible for this. Looking back, years later, she knew she had experienced a panic attack (her first). Sister Lucia had been kind and did not chastise her for doing something wrong. From that day forward, no aerosol cans were deposited in the metal drum. Sister Vincent used a box beside the trash can. She also burned half the trash at a time - once in the morning, then once in the afternoon.

Soon it was October and the Novices would finally see their families again. The day was cloudy; it looked like it might rain. This year, Florence and her two boys, drove to Parkland County with one of the other Novice's parents who lived in the same neighborhood. Sister Vincent seemed more reserved this year. Her mother was worried about her. The happy-go-lucky daughter of last year was not there. Florence had bought pinking shears for Sister Vincent who liked to make special cards to send home. She had also asked for a calligraphy pen and ink. That was not forthcoming this time around.

In December, most of her fellow Novices changed work assignments. The only ones who did not change jobs were the sewing room Novices and Sister Vincent. She remained in the laundry with even more responsibility for cleaning the coat room with all their rain boots. Once a week she had to clean the Recreation room as well.

Christmas visitation from parents and family occurred in the Recreation Room on a Saturday afternoon. It was a good time. Parents always seemed to bring a variety of baked goods and boxes of chocolate candy. Most of the edibles went to the Infirmary to be stored; Sister Lucia doled it out in the evenings to follow. The St. Louis chocolate truffles were everybody's favorite. Sister Vincent's mother had baked a pie and brownies and Christmas butter cookies. It was a feast. She also received the calligraphy pen and black ink she wanted. Her mother went searching for a small needle nosed pliers that could be used to bend wires to make long rosary beads. Sister Vincent was happy with her gifts.

The winter was cold with a few inches of snow in December and January. One February morning, the bell rang as usual - dressing, and bathroom tasks followed. Sister Vincent was usually the first one down to the coat room to leave to walk the Rosary path over to the main convent. This particular morning, Sister Lucia was in the coat room, and told the Novices to report to the chapel on the second floor. There had been an overnight snowstorm with 18 inches of the white flakes surrounding the Novitiate. The trees were covered in white. It looked like a fairy land. They would not be able to get over to the main convent. Novices were in the chapel for an hour. The postulants were in their community room in silence for an hour. Then they proceeded down to the basement to the Recreation room. There, small boxes of dry cereal flakes were distributed. They just about had enough for everyone. The morning was spent in the trunk room first and then in their cells (small room). It was a cleaning morning.

By 11:00 am Rosary path had been plowed as well as the exit from the Novitiate. They reported to the main chapel for noontime prayers. They then had to do all their chores in the afternoon. It was a very rare exception to the monotony of the daily schedule. Even Sister Vincent was happy for the distraction. It was like an adventure they would remember for years to come.

With March came longer days and more sunlight to melt the snow. In April at Easter time, the Novices spent a week on Retreat. There were lectures every day by a travelling retreat priest. He was an eloquent speaker and kept them engaged. The priest spoke about their dedication to the Catholic Church and its mission. He spoke about the value of meditation. He spoke about the vows of poverty, chastity and obedience. There was no recreation for the entire week. It was a solemn week for the Novices about to profess their vows for one year.

Along came May with the flowering dogwood trees. Profession Day loomed.

Another transition would be made. In addition to reciting the three vows, one-by-one, to the Mother General, they would replace the white veil with a stiff black veil. This ceremony was very formal with all of the Novices lying prostate on the marble floor in front of the postulant stalls. Sister Vincent was consumed with sadness for some unknown reason. She had been feeling nervous or anxious for weeks before this ceremony. She really did not want to leave the Novitiate. In hindsight, she felt safe in that building. She had also been singled out for a job of responsibility. That was a good feeling. The unknown made her fearful. She was crying as she lied on the floor face down. In order of rank each Novice got up and knelt before the Mother General and recited her vows for one year. Sister Vincent managed to stop the tears; her eyes were all red. She said her vows and went back to the sacristy to trade her veil. When the rest of the ceremony was over, they processed out of the chapel to the grassy area around the lake.

These brand-new nuns were again with their families. The tone of the day was more reverent than the jubilation of a year ago. Sister Vincent did not really feel like celebrating. She put up a good front while pictures were taken. Her life as a nun was just beginning.

CHAPTER 8

Professed Vows

These newly professed nuns had a new Superior. She was the head of the main convent (the Motherhouse). After Matins that first night, Sister Vincent and her "band" (class), went out onto the large screened porch of the main convent for an hour of recreation. The living arrangements for May, June and July had changed. The new nuns were back on the first floor of the Novitiate again. In August, they would receive their first assignment from the Mother General. For the summer they would attend college taking a variety of courses, including Art, Astronomy, Philosophy of Education, and/or Calculus.

During the second week after her profession, Sister Vincent did not feel well. She felt sick to her stomach and very nervous. She stood in line outside the Superior's Office to ask for permission to go back to bed. Sister Vincent did not know what was wrong with her – she just didn't feel well enough to go on. Years later, she would come to know it was a mental health issue. Perhaps, she felt abandoned by Sister Zachariah. Sister Vincent had not seen her for three years. Unfortunately, appropriate care was not forthcoming. Sister Lucia brought her something to eat in the gloomy dormitory. The rest of her band was watching a movie for the first time in three years.

Her first summer assignment was with a group of 18 young boys, seven-years old. They were her "charges". A new routine was established. Sister Sarah, her old Novice mother, was working with the same group of boys. She showed Sister Vincent the ins and outs of caring for this group of youngsters living in an open dormitory in the oldest part of the main building.

Sister Vincent had to wake up the seven-year old boys at 7 am. She helped them dress with clean underwear provided and then line them up for breakfast. The boys' dining room was in the dungeon. She had to serve them breakfast at long tables and cajole the boy who did not want to eat. The nuns were providing what today is known as foster care. There were ten groups of twenty or so boys. The ages ranged from 6 to 14. A school was in a smaller building on the campus. Older retired nuns taught at this school.

At 9:00 am, Sister Vincent had to be at the college for the Astronomy course she was enrolled in. Every other day she attended the noon prayers in the main chapel. Other days she took her group of boys to lunch in their dining room. Recess followed out in a large field behind the school building. School for the boys was in session all summer. In the evenings after Matins, she had to give up her recreation to get the young boys settled into the dormitory. Usually there was a movie for them watch as a group.

When the sultry days of August rolled around, most of these

newly professed nuns were on pins and needles. They awaited "the list" assigning them somewhere. Most of the band went out to parishes in the New York City area to teach even though they did not yet have their Bachelor's degree. Some of the convents were large with 12 to 16 nuns teaching in the parish school. Some of the convents were small with only six nuns teaching in a smaller school.

Sister Vincent was one of twelve nuns assigned to stay at the Motherhouse and work with a group of boys. She was attending college full time now. Chemistry and Physics was her class load during the week, and Education courses were on Friday nights and all-day Saturday. The living arrangements for these 12 nuns was up on the fourth floor of the aged primary building. There was very little heat. Most of them shared a room. The evenings after 9 pm were spent doing homework. Sister Vincent had problem sets to solve and Lab reports for both sciences once a week. She was finding it difficult to keep up with the work. It was a hectic schedule: prayers, a group of boys to attend to, and college classes.

In September, she had a postulant to help take care of the group with her. But the postulant's time was limited. During Vespers, every other day, Sister Vincent was assigned to the field where the boys rough housed together. She had to keep the peace and get them downstairs for supper. The professed nuns took turns supervising with a whistle; the large dining hall seated 200 boys.

Once a week in the evening, the boys were led to a large shower room with no privacy for the boys. The showers were at the end of "rat alley". It was still dark and dungy. They used their towels to march back upstairs to the dormitory to get dressed in clean clothes provided for them – pajamas, jeans, shirts, underwear, socks and sneakers. Each boy had a locker out in the corridor of the dormitory. Supervision of the boys was difficult for Sister Vincent. She really did not like the job.

And, so the year continued through the Fall when in October the families visited again. This visit was a lonely one. Sister Vincent was walking around the Fair by herself. Her mother had given her $5.00 the previous afternoon. There was a nun at a table offering handwriting analysis. Sister Vincent gave her a dollar and proceeded to copy the two sentences in her best penmanship. When she finished writing, the nun told her to come back in an hour. Sister Vincent continued to feel dejected by her work load. However, when she received the report of her hand-writing analysis, for the first time in her life she read about positive qualities. She was a leader, a take-charge person, precise with detail, and very sincere and empathetic. She was shocked to have her great work ethic finally validated.

Her self-esteem grew that day.

Her assignment to take care of the group of boys continued into the Spring.

Easter week came with another yearly retreat. She had some relief from the burden of caring for the boys. The postulant assumed most of their care with time off for Sister Vincent. The boys saw their families once a month. Some boys saw no one. They were given ice cream as a treat.

In August of 1963, Sister Vincent was assigned to a convent in Parkland County. There, the Superior, an elderly woman with an accent, told her she would have a third-grade class. That particular class had a special needs student who happened to be the son of the secretary of the school.

PART III

CHAPTER 9

Teaching

*S*ister Vincent's college classes in Philosophy and Psychology of Education did not prepare her for teaching reading to this third grade class of thirty-two students. She was using a color-coded Reading program known as a curriculum with groups of four and five students at different levels of comprehension. Some of the students were above third grade level. Some of the students were below third grade reading level. Attention was given to the group of low-level readers.

After breakfast, she hurriedly swept the staircase in this new convent building. Then proceeded to the classroom to write on the blackboard questions about the reading assignment for the low-level readers. It was a tense job for her. Third graders were still fidgety to some extent. Care of little ones did not seem to be her forte.

So, she was in the classroom from 8 am until 2:45 pm. Once a week she missed the main meal at noon. She was outside supervising recess for the whole school. She ate dinner quickly after the other nuns finished dinner and one of them relieved her outside. Sister Vincent was assigned by the Superior to give piano lessons to young students from the school. The lessons started at 3 pm and lasted until 5 pm.

This occurred four days a week in the sun parlor in the basement of the convent with a back door for entrance. The lessons were 30 minutes each and the cost was $5.00 a lesson. By the end of the week, Sister Vincent had accumulated $80. When she turned this over to the Superior, the old nun would chide Sister Vincent if there was less than $80. All of the other teaching nuns were free from 3 to 5 pm to correct unending papers from the students or take a nap.

And so, her workday ended in time for Vespers chanting in the little chapel, followed by supper (a light meal). Chapel followed again for Matins chanting and a hymn that Sister Vincent had to play on the organ. Correcting of her class papers occurred during the hour of recreation in the Community Room with a television. This was the first access to TV that she had in four years. On rare occasions, the five younger nuns mostly from her band, would sneak down to the Community Room around 11 pm to watch a movie. It was not without fear that the Superior would appear and proceed to punish them - no dessert for a week.

In January of 1964, Sister Vincent's assignment changed. She took over a fifth-grade class that a lay teacher left in a lurch. Her classroom was on the second floor now. Fifth graders knew how to read and write at this point. They now studied new subjects: geography, and history, in addition to English, math, and religion. They were a friendly group of youngsters. Sister Vincent had more papers to correct now. She also had greater preparation for her class. After two months of settling the students into a new routine, her Education supervisor, a nun from the college, came to observe her teach for the whole morning. Sister Vincent was a nervous wreck. Apparently, it went well; she received no negative feedback. She was unaware of her innate abilities.

To make matters worse, the five youngest nuns piled into a station wagon to go over to the college for a Friday night class with another class on Saturday. They would drive back to the parish convent by 3 pm Saturday. Then, if they were lucky, they could wash and press their clothes and/or clean their cell. At least each nun had a room to themselves. It contained a comfortable bed, a sink with running water, a desk with a chair and lamp, and a closet to hang their habits. This was the first real privacy that the young nuns had.

The summer rolled around, a predictable "summer assignments" list came in the mail. All of the younger nuns were assigned to a Summer Camp far out on Long Island, New York. It was another money-maker for the Motherhouse. There were 6 cabins of 15 children. Two nuns were assigned to each cabin. There was a small room for them to sleep in while minding their "charges". There was a dining hall and kitchen. There was a swimming pool. There was a field for playing baseball or softball. Every two weeks the children would go home on Monday morning in buses. On Tuesday afternoon a new group arrived from New York City. The break in their schedule allowed the nuns to use the pool and play softball. A few of them had guitars. It was the age of folk music. Radios at the camp played most of these folk songs. The nuns loved the songs, although they did not know all the political implications of the songs. It was the age of the Civil Rights movement.

As professed nuns now, they were allowed two weeks of vacation on a piece of land that this religious community owned north of Parkland County. It abutted the Hudson River. Rules were relaxed. They attended a Mass in the morning in a make-shift chapel. Breakfast was served to them. Then, they made peanut butter and jelly sandwiches to last the rest of the day. Some of the young nuns, during the last two weeks of August, had brought snacks with them. They feasted on pretzels, potato chips, Cheetos, and peanuts. Those "snack" nuns had a lax superior who allowed them to go to the grocery store and buy all the snacks. During this vacation, Sister Vincent was assigned to sleep in a cottage a mile away from the other buildings. The beds were lumpy; the cabin was damp; the air was humid; the windows did not open. Mosquitoes abounded; the small cabin never got sunlight; it was not an ideal place to sleep.

Near the main building was a steep path that lead down to a dock on the river. There were three row boats and a wooden shack for changing in and out of bathing suits. The dock was crowded from 10 am 'til 5 pm. Sunbathing was enormously popular. No one knew the dangers of UV radiation at that time. The goal of most was to return to their parish convents with a dark tan. Rainy days were boring. Almost all of these young nuns crowded into the main sleeping quarters building. It was a dark place with overhead light bulbs suspended from the ceiling. Some of the nuns opted to wear their habits and walk back up the path for a real dinner and supper.

And so, Sister Vincent's first year of teaching ended with an assignment to return to the same convent and parish school.

CHAPTER 10

Science Teacher

*I*n September 1964, Sister Vincent was back at the same parish convent and school. It was located north of the City in Parkland County. The Superior gave her a different assignment. She was moving up to a 7th grade classroom. She would be teaching Science and Geography to the two 7th grade classes and the two eighth grade classes. It was a rotating schedule with forty-five minutes for Science and the same for Geography. The other three nuns taught Math, English, Reading and History. That added up to 4.5 hours of instruction for each of the four classes.

Since it was 1964, Sputnik had been launched, and now the importance of Science education took center stage. It was new to the curriculum. The 7th graders would learn the basics of Life Science. The 8th graders would learn about Matter and Energy. Science was Sister Vincent's background; she was happy to be teaching what she really loved. Geography turned out to be fun for her, also. The 7th graders learned all about the geography of North, Central, and

South America. The 8th graders learned all about the geography specifics of New York State – a somewhat boring course of study.

The difficulty for Sister Vincent arose because of the piano lessons after school coupled with college classes on Friday night and all-day Saturday. She had very little time for such a workload. And, please remember, all the work was "pro bono". She never saw a penny nor were compensations paid to Social Security.

The Dean of the college, summoned Sister Vincent to her office one Saturday morning. She was due to graduate in June and the Dean indicated she was short 2 credits. Therefore, Sister Martin would teach her Genetics for 4 credits the first semester. Then, she would teach her Biochemistry for 4 credits the second semester. Sister Vincent liked Sister Martin who was rotund and quite knowledgeable. Sister Martin liked Sister Vincent when she noticed her aptitude for detailed work.

One day in October, Sister Martin told Sister Vincent that 3M was sponsoring a contest for overhead transparencies. She wondered whether Sister Vincent could draw a representative animal for each of the phyla. Naturally she agreed to do this. Sister Martin procured all the materials for her – clear acetate films, colored ink pens and a portfolio. Sister Vincent had six weeks to complete the drawings.

She used a college Biology book to copy each of the animals freehand including an amoeba, mollusk, crayfish, spider, bird, fish, ending with a mammal. All in all, there were twelve drawings. She did the drawings first on white paper then on an acetate film. Sister Vincent did these tedious labelled drawings at night on the floor of her cell. She would fall dead asleep at 11:30 pm. One night she never made it into her bed. She fell asleep on her knees with her head resting on the bed! She did finish them in time. She submitted her work to Sister Martin one Saturday in late November, just before Thanksgiving. Sister Martin was astounded at the perfection of each drawing. Sister Vincent had done exactly what she was good at – layout and design. These particular skills she would use later in her life.

With Sister Martin, there was an experiment she had to do with fireflies. First, the firefly needed to be anesthetized with ether. It entailed injecting the firefly with a dye so that the glow from its abdomen would be phosphorescent. Sister Vincent was learning new techniques that would be useful in the future. Genetics, during the first semester, was easy enough. Biochemistry she found more difficult. Sister Martin was a patient teacher. The final exam topics she knew ahead of time. Sister Vincent went ahead and memorized the Krebs cycle and the names of all organic molecules. Sister Martin gave her two A's for 8 credits.

One weekend during the Spring of 1965, she arrived at the college at 6:30 pm on a Friday evening for an Education Seminar. As she climbed the stairs she once had to clean as a postulant, there was a bulletin board hanging on the wall on the landing. There was a Parkland County newspaper article with front-page headlines: "Sister Martin Wins Top Prize in 3M Contest". Sister Vincent was flabbergasted. Her drawings won first prize – a fully paid vacation to Mexico. Her heart was pounding with elation. None of her peers knew of the honor she received. This would remain a "feather in her in cap" forever.

In May, Sister Gregory summoned Sister Vincent to her office again. Sister Gregory conveyed a message from the Mother General. Since she had not taken Final Vows yet, she would not be able to travel to Mexico with Sister Martin. Sister Vincent was saddened for this lack of recognition that she rightly deserved. In class the next morning, Sister Martin was so apologetic as well as grateful to this young nun who had done such a superb job with her drawings. The 3M Company would reproduce them and sell them with their new overhead projectors.

The Dean planned the June graduation ceremony to be held in a tent on the college grounds. The Dean informed Sister Vincent that she missed a cum Laude diploma by only one-hundreth of a point. Another bitter disappointment for her because she had completed all the Education course projects to the letter. A particular Education Methods instructor was mentally unstable and gave Sister Vincent only a C for six credits. Obviously, those C grades hurt her academic record. She would carry a resentment against that Education instructor nun for years.

To make matters worse again, Sister Vincent's mother, Florence, criticized her vociferously after the ceremony. Why hadn't she graduated with Honors, like two of her classmates? Sister Vincent thought she was back in high school again when her mother criticized her report cards. At least, she had her Bachelor Degree in Science Education, as well as Certification from the State of New York to teach Grades K – 8. Thus, another teaching year came to an end. Her summer assignment was to teach the Chemistry Lab at the college. It would definitely be a challenge for her.

CHAPTER 11

After Graduation

*S*ister Vincent stayed on at the same school. It was 1965. Three of her classmates were assigned elsewhere. Newly professed nuns came to take their place. Her assignments were the same: science and geography for the two seventh grade classes and the two eighth grade classes. Piano lessons continued after school.

She had graduated from the college in June, so that eliminated the weekly trip to the college on Friday afternoons and all-day Saturday. Sister Vincent had her driver's license now, and frequently had to take the Superior to see her cardiologist. Other driving assignments were also given to her. Each convent usually had one or two designated drivers.

The academic year progressed smoothly for the most part. One Saturday in that Spring of 1966, Sister Vincent was told to accompany an older nun on a visit to her family at 1:00 pm. Another rule reigned: they would not travel alone but always in pairs. She was also the driver for this nun. It seemed like a long afternoon to

Sister Vincent. They did not have to return to the convent until 7 pm.

Sister Teresa's family was friendly enough and insisted that Sister Vincent have some 7-Up. They re-filled her glass when it was empty. What she did not know was that there was Vodka mixed with the 7-Up. She had three or four glasses in the course of the afternoon. Sister Theresa's family had succeeded in getting both of the nuns drunk. It would have been funny except Sister Vincent had to get behind the wheel of a station wagon and drive 30 miles home. It was a scary venture for this young nun who white knuckled that steering wheel while driving drunk in traffic on Interstate 95 at 65 mph.

Sister Vincent's summer assignment was back at the college as a Chemistry Lab instructor. When August 15th rolled around the new assignments were posted. Sister Vincent wasn't going anywhere. But, to her shock, Sister Zachariah was assigned to the same convent and school. She really had no idea what to expect. At the most, Sister Vincent had seen Sister Zachariah only briefly on two or three occasions in the past six years. Their old sacristy friendly relationship was non-existent.

Sister Zachariah was due to arrive during the afternoon of the Saturday of Labor Day weekend. It was the same day that Sister Vincent had been assigned to cook dinner for the community of 14. All she remembered for a long time was how anxious she felt. She was cooking spaghetti sauce from scratch and making meatballs also. She was doing exactly what her mother had taught her. It took Sister Vincent almost the whole day to cook the meatballs and sauce from scratch.

By 4:00 pm everything was in order in the kitchen. The doorbell rang at 4:30 pm. There she was! She smiled at Sister Vincent. There was no warmth or other recognition given. Sister Zachariah asked, "Where is the Superior?" Sister Vincent told her to go the top of the stairs on the second floor. There she would find the Superior's office. She was then assigned a bedroom (cell) directly across from Sister Vincent, by chance. Sister Vincent helped her carry her suitcases up the stairs to the second floor and down the hallway near the end of the corridor.

Vespers was at 5 pm in the small chapel on the first floor across from the refectory. Sister Vincent was excused by the Superior to cook all the spaghetti. She was responsible for bringing the serving bowls to the head of the table to the Superior. All 14 nuns sat in order of rank. Sister Zachariah was two seats down from the Superior at the long table; Sister Vincent was 5 seats down from the head of the table on the same side as her mentor.

Chanting of Matins followed at 6 pm with the singing of the hymn, Salve Regina. Sister Vincent was still responsible for playing the little electric organ. Recreation followed in the Community room down the hallway from the refectory. Long rectangular tables had chairs and there were no assigned seats. Sister Zachariah had been assigned to manage one of the eighth grade classes and then rotate among the two seventh grade classes and two eighth grade classes to teach English as well as Reading. Sister Zachariah by this time had become a "reading specialist".

Classes were scheduled to start at 9:00 am on Tuesday. Monday was Labor Day. Most of the nuns spent part of the holiday in their classroom counting textbooks, writing names in the Attendance

Register, and posting signs with directions for fire drills, for lunch times, and for recess times. It was a day off for Sister Vincent because she had everything in order and ready to go. She visited Sister Zachariah's classroom to see if she needed any help. Sister Vincent spent some of her afternoon counting textbooks for Sister Zachariah. There had still not been any friendly banter between them. That left Sister Vincent confused about their relationship. It was probably due to the "particular friendship" rule that existed. It was to be avoided at all costs.

School started and Sister Vincent had little spare time with four classes of science to teach and then four classes of geography. As a matter of fact, one of those eighth-grade classes, had sixty students on the roster. Yes, that's right, 60 students – 6 crowded vertical rows with 10 students per row. Her schedule, including piano lessons from 3 pm to 5 pm, had not changed. Thanks to Sister Martin, her Professor at the college, Sister Vincent had applied for an NSF grant to participate in a Graduate Geology course held on Saturday mornings from 8:30 am – 12:30 pm. Her letter of acceptance had arrived in August. Sister Vincent's Superior consulted with the Mother General and gave permission for Sister Vincent to take the course. She was excited at the prospect of getting graduate credit for a Geology course. Perhaps someday she would have her Master's degree.

CHAPTER 12

Graduate School

Unknown to Sister Vincent, Sister Zachariah had enrolled in a graduate course in Reading Methods at another College on Saturday mornings. When Sister Vincent asked the Superior for bus and subway fares on Friday evening, she gave her a five-dollar bill. Then, this very old nun told her she would not be travelling alone. Sister Zachariah was to be her companion on the bus ride into the City followed by the subway ride downtown.

Sister Vincent, now aware of Sister Zachariah's graduate course, knew that her college was in the opposite direction from hers. Both nuns went to chapel Saturday morning at 6 am for the chanting of Lauds. After the chanting, they were excused to get some coffee and breakfast cereal. The walk to the bus stop took 7-8 minutes. The first City bus was at 7 am. It was going to be a warm, sunny, fall day as the sun rose over the bus stop.

Sister Zachariah got on the nearly empty bus first; she was followed by Sister Vincent. The older nun took a seat by a window toward the back of the bus. Since they were travelling companions, Sister Vincent sat next to her in the aisle seat.

As the bus driver drove south toward the city, Sister Zachariah placed her right thigh up against Sister Vincent's left thigh. Sister Vincent moved slightly to the right to protect her personal space. Immediately Sister Zachariah moved her leg to touch this younger nun again. Sister Vincent felt something like an electrical shock go through her body. She did not have any idea what was happening to her. However, Sister Vincent just automatically returned the pressure from her thigh to Sister Zachariah's thigh. The very pleasant feeling in her lower body persisted and seemed to grow stronger. Sister Vincent did not know how to identify it at all.

This experience and feeling ended when they got off the bus at the Bus Terminal. They went down to the subway and caught the express A train. There was no physical contact between the two of them. It was clear to Sister Vincent while they were sitting facing other passengers; touching would have been obvious and also unusual.

They exited the train and the two of them parted ways. Sister Vincent caught a D train heading south. She was on her way to her first graduate class. She was very familiar with this area because she had worked there for a year after graduation from high school. At the University building she followed the arrows up to the third floor. She barely had time to use the Restroom before 8:30 am. The lecture hall was filled with 30 students.

There was a seat in the front row of this lecture hall that suited Sister Vincent just fine. She had a new notebook and the Professor gave each of them a new Geology textbook. There was no tuition and no charge for the textbook because this class was funded by the National Science Foundation (NSF) as a grant to the University. In this age of "Sputnik", as it was called in the early 60s, there was a generous amount of government money available to further the education of science teachers.

During a break from the lecture, Sister Vincent noticed two other nuns wearing the same habit as she was. They were from the same religious community in Parkland County. Sister Vincent smiled at the two nuns as she stood up from seat. They introduced themselves; they were science teachers from a high school in the Bronx. They joked with her about her easy 8th grade workload compared to their demanding high school schedule.

When class was over, Sister Vincent headed out to the subway for her trip back to the 59th Street subway station. Although it was a warm day near 80 degrees, the nuns had to wear a heavy, black, sleeveless cloak (a mantle) over their habit. At the train station she met Sister Zachariah for the commute home. Sister Vincent waited for Sister Zachariah to appear off a southbound subway train. Together, they climbed the stairs to the lobby and down another flight of stairs to the northbound side of the tracks.

It was 1:15 pm when they arrived back at the bus station. The same routine as the morning ensued. Only this time, sitting in a comfortable seat Sister Vincent realized how tired she was. Adrenaline will do that to a person. Sister Zachariah's thigh found Sister Vincent's under their mantles. It was not quite as exciting nor as intense as the morning bus ride. It was after 2:00 pm when they arrived back at the convent.

CHAPTER 13

The Sponsor

*D*uring the course of the next week Sister Vincent found reasons to knock on Sister Zachariah's door to ask her some kind of a question. Visiting another nun's cell was forbidden after 9:00 pm. Sister Vincent found herself wanting to chat with her sponsor. Perhaps she was trying to establish the friendly relationship that had existed back in the sacristy when she was twelve years old. She was now twenty-two years old. Sister Zachariah was thirty-five years old.

Of course, there was no mention of the Saturday morning bus ride in their conversations. Sister Zachariah knew exactly what she was doing. She was sexually attracted to Sister Vincent; just as she had been all those years ago in the sacristy of the Church. Many years later, hindsight for Sister Vincent became 20/20. However, it was very obvious to Sister Zachariah at the present time that Sister Vincent had absolutely no knowledge of what was happening to her. Sexual arousal never occurred in Sister Vincent's life up until now.

The next Saturday rolled around quickly. The same ritual ensued for the second time. Sister Vincent was not the initiator of the physical contact as they sat on the bus. Sister Zachariah wanted to physically feel this young nun. The same feelings engulfed Sister Vincent when Sister Zachariah exerted pressure on her left thigh. She felt no pain or she would have moved to another seat in the bus. It all felt good to her albeit foreign. The bus ride ended all too quickly.

As if nothing happened, the nuns rode the subway into Manhattan. Sister Vincent changed southbound trains and was headed to her second class. She truly enjoyed learning new information. She took to a classroom like a duck to water. An undergraduate Earth Science course helped her immensely. It was one of her favorites. What she was learning about geology as well as the hands-on activities they performed with minerals and rocks improved her teaching skills now and in the future.

Her new relationship with Sister Zachariah was progressing although lop-sided. It was Sister Vincent who was assuming the role of a care giver. She had learned this well in her family of origin. As a youngster she took care of her mother, then Gerard, and finally Tyler. As an example, Sister Vincent washed Sister Zachariah's clothes, dried and folded them. One day, Sister Vincent felt neglected and right there in the laundry room blurted out to Sister Zachariah, "You have no idea how I feel." Oh, yes, Sister Zachariah understood perfectly.

It was Sister Vincent now becoming attracted and attached to Sister Zachariah, although the feelings were still somewhat of an enigma to Sister Vincent. It became obvious to the other two older nuns working with them in the rotation of the seventh and eighth grades, that a "particular friendship" had developed between Sister Zachariah and Sister Vincent. Sister Zachariah seemed to be the aggressor; she was very outspoken about teaching and the reading equipment she wanted. The other two nuns spoke to each of them only when necessary and then quite formally. This was the only way they knew how to express disapproval. Nothing was ever spoken about their "particular friendship" expressly forbidden by the vow of chastity they had taken.

One Saturday in November, Sister Vincent arrived at the subway station about 1:00 pm to wait for Sister Zachariah as she always did. Fifteen minutes passed. By the time 30 minutes passed, Sister Vincent was pacing back and forth – the entire length of the platform. She was close to a panic attack after 55 minutes. Where could she be? This woman with whom she was emotionally attached suddenly appeared! Sister Vincent wanted to hug her and cry. All she uttered was, "Where have you been all this time?" Totally unsympathetic Sister Zachariah replied, "I was talking with two other students after the class - no big deal." Sister Vincent once again received no validation of her feelings. She lived by the mantra she had learned from her mother, "What is WRONG with you?" Subconsciously, Sister Vincent believed there was something wrong with her.

So, the bus rides continued through October, November, and into early December. The physical contact continued on the bus, and Sister Vincent just accepted this. She came to enjoy it. Then it ended after final exams in December. During February, somehow Sister Zachariah convinced that same grouchy Superior that a trip to New York City on the northeast corridor of a New York Central train was an excellent field trip for all the eighth grade students. Exactly how Sister Zachariah procured the permission from the Superior, all the information for the morning trains, a Statue of Liberty visit, as well as the top of the Empire State Building visit was a mystery to Sister Vincent. She was not privy to the plans for the trip. Basically, she had no input into the designs of this excursion.

Honestly, Sister Vincent was wishing that an older nun would accompany Sister Zachariah. Of course, Sister Zachariah would hear of no such thing. There would be two parents with the two nuns. The younger nun truly did not feel comfortable always being pulled into plans of the older nun. Sister Vincent acutely remembers that long train ride into the City. She chose to sit by herself. She was experiencing severe cramps that accompanied her monthly period. However, she was always inspired by the Grand Central Station on East 42nd Street. The myriad of train tracks and switches including the many other tunnels for pedestrians to find alternate New York City subway trains left her in awe. The historic building was cavernous with train tracks on two different levels.

Her father had taught her the history of Grand Central when she was 11 years old. It opened in 1913, built on the site of two predecessor stations dating back to 1871. It was built by and also named, "The New York Central Railroad". The majestic architecture and interior design of the Terminal is remarkable; it is included as a National Historic Landmark.

Grand Central, as it is now known, covers 48 acres of space. It has 44 platforms, more than any other railroad station in the world. These platforms, all *below* ground, serve 30 tracks on the upper level and 26 on the lower. Of these, 43 tracks are in use for passenger service day in and day out. Two dozen more serve as a rail yard and sidings for unused older trains. Currently another eight tracks and four platforms are being built on two new levels deep underneath the existing station – a project to be completed in the 2020s. It will service what is known as the Long Island Railroad.

It turned out to be a grueling trip with grave responsibility for so many young adolescents. Two parents, Mrs. Davey and Mrs. Kebbey, accompanied them to help with supervision. Both of these women had daughters in the eighth grade. It was a cold, and cloudy day. The ferry ride across the mouth of the Hudson River brought them to the base of the Statue of Liberty. Most of the students climbed the narrow metal steps to the very top of Lady Liberty. After another ferry ride back to Battery Park, they paused there long enough to eat their bagged lunches.

From there they took a subway ride north to 34th Street and walked east to the Empire State building on 5th Avenue. The students were in groups of twenty and took an express elevator to the indoor Observation Deck. Many of the students used the mounted binoculars to view surrounding areas. A few students saw birds flying past them. It was an interesting adventure for most of the adolescents. If Sister Vincent had had *her druthers,* she would have chosen the Museum of Natural History for this field trip. There is so much science related information there. After lunch in the Museum's cafeteria, a New York Planetarium show could have followed.

By 4 o'clock, they all walked back to the Grand Central Terminal to board a train headed north along the east side of the Hudson River. They disembarked at the Marymount Station where parents waited for their children. Mrs. Davey was happy to drive the two nuns back to the convent across the Tappan Zee Bridge. Sister Zachariah and Mrs. Davey formed a bond on that trip during their seven hours together. This was a relationship that Sister Zachariah manipulated for the rest of the year. She depended on Mrs. Davey to drive her whenever and wherever she wanted.

CHAPTER 14

A Nightmare

Although there was no more ritual physical contact between Sister Zachariah and Sister Vincent, the younger nun continued to care for her sponsor. She visited her cell daily to see if she needed anything. Then one night an egregious offense occurred. Sister Vincent awoke in the middle of the night. What occurred was a nightmare.

Without a speck of rational thinking, she got out of her bed in a nightgown, walked across the hall, and entered Sister Zachariah's cell. As she climbed into bed with this older nun, Sister Zachariah had pulled back her blanket and welcomed her with open arms. Her sponsor said not a single word to discourage what was about to happen. Sister Vincent automatically moved on top of Sister Zachariah. It was as if there was a force driving her to rub her pubic area on Sister Zachariah's knee until there was an incredible release of physical energy. Sister Vincent was shocked at what just happened. It was the first time she ever felt something quite so powerful. She promptly removed herself from this room, even though Sister Zachariah said, "Stay". Sister Vincent went back to her own cell.

Sister Vincent was beside herself. She had no name for what had just happened, but there was no doubt in her mind she had just committed a mortal sin! Now, what was she going to do about that? Her mind was racing. It was 1:35 am. She was extremely anxious, worried, and confused. If ever there was a quagmire, this was one of them. There was no sleep for this young woman. What had happened? Why had she done this? Please recall that the only "sex education" Sister Vincent received was out of a college biology textbook. She did remember discovering her clitoris one day taking a bath when she was eleven years old. At that time, she had no idea what it might be. When this occurred, she never spoke about it to her mother who was pregnant for the fourth time.

The morning bell rang, Sister Vincent got dressed and went down to the chapel for the chanting of Lauds. Her stomach felt queasy, the muscles in her arms were quivering ever so slightly, and her brain felt funny probably from lack of sleep. After chanting, the nuns sat for 30 minutes of meditation.

Her mind was still racing. How in the world was she to get absolution for her mortal sin? This commission precluded her from receiving Holy Communion during the Mass that followed. So, as the rest of the nuns processed to the altar, Sister Vincent stood to let two of the nuns in her row pass by. How mortifying was that. Hopefully they would think that she had gone into the kitchen and eaten some food. What else were they to think?

Being incredibly dishonest, Sister Zachariah feigned illness;

she never reported to the chapel for prayers and Mass or the refectory for breakfast. Poor Sister Vincent could not swallow the scrambled eggs on her plate. She was the first one up from the table. She washed her plate, fork, and coffee cup, returned them to the table and rushed to get over to the school. There was a pay phone at the end of the long first floor hallway. She made a collect call to her brother at his Seminary across the Hudson River. When the operator got him to the phone, Sister Vincent pleaded with her brother to please ask Monsignor Peters to visit her at the convent at 3:00 pm. She had come up with this feasible solution while sitting during meditation.

Her brother, John, had introduced her to Monsignor Peters when she visited the Seminary last year. Permission from the Mother General let her visit John once a year. Monsignor Peters was a short man with red piping around his long cassock. He was warm, congenial and interested in her position at the school teaching science. He seemed to be the only priest whom Sister Vincent thought she could ask for absolution of her mortal sin.

She went to her classroom on the second floor of the school and sat at her desk. In her mind, she asked how she was ever going to get through this ominous day of teaching eight different classes? Trying to function normally without sleep for the first time in her life, seemed insurmountable. At 8:30 am she stood in the hallway as students were at their lockers. Adjacent to Sister Vincent's seventh grade classroom was Sister Zachariah's eighth grade classroom. Sister Zachariah appeared after skipping prayers and breakfast. When she walked over to Sister Vincent and asked, "Are you OK"?

Sister Vincent replied, "No, I am not!" She promptly walked away and went back inside with the seventh graders.

In all of the science and geography classes Sister Vincent was able to assign the students questions out of their textbooks She expected the finished written answers tomorrow. She was then able to sit at the desk in the four classrooms and rest her very weary body. As 2:45 pm approached, Sister Vincent was anxious and very nervous all over again.

Sister Vincent was back at the convent by 3:00 pm. She waited in her cell, door open, listening for the doorbell. When it rang about 3:10 pm, she opened the door and proceeded to bring Monsignor Peters into the small square room called a parlor where the nuns met visitors. Sister Vincent thanked him profusely for coming over the Tappan Zee Bridge to see her. He noticed her pale face and said, "What happened to you?" Sister Vincent blurted out, "I went into my sponsor's room last night and I need absolution for what I did." He said, "All right." There were no questions asked. Sister Vincent was so much relieved. He took out a little purple strip of a stole and hung it around his neck. In Latin he granted her absolution from her mortal sin! He told her to go say five Our Father prayers. This was known as a penance to the one absolved of all sin.

Surprisingly, Monsignor Peters asked her to go get the other nun involved in the situation. Sister Zachariah did not want to go down to see him. Sister Vincent said coldly, "He wants to see you!" What then transpired between those two, she would never know. All of this occurred in early May. The school year was coming to an end! Sister Vincent no longer went into Sister Zachariah's cell every afternoon. Nor did she ask her any questions. Her contact with this person was diminished as well as the emotions she once felt for her.

One evening in early June, about 9:15 pm, there was a knock at her door. Lo and behold, Sister Zachariah was standing there, and walked uninvited into Sister Vincent's cell. Sister Zachariah took Sister Vincent's hand into her own. She held them up and said, "Do you really think that there is something wrong with this?" Sister Vincent yanked her hand away and said, "Yes, I most certainly do. Now, get out." Sister Zachariah's response was, "I think you are making a big mistake. There is absolutely nothing wrong with this." How unbalanced was this older person who had exerted so much power over Sister Vincent?

There was no doubt in Sister Vincent's mind about her response. She was still confused, but the end-of-the-year workload distracted her from this unfortunate turn of events. Her summer assignment was to teach the Chemistry Lab for the college's General Chemistry 1. It was also the summer of Sister Vincent's final vows on August 15th. Sister Vincent looked forward to being reunited with her band (class) and family that day. They were six years older now; most of them were experienced teachers.

Meanwhile, Sister Zachariah went ahead and made plans for a trip to the Long Island shore to visit with her sister and brother-in-law for a week's vacation. She told Sister Vincent that the Mother General said she was to be her companion. The arrangements included the time-consuming drive to Long Island donated by Mr. and Mrs. Davey from the parish. Sister Vincent in her heart did not want to go and spend a week with strangers and Sister Zachariah. She resented being pulled away right after the Final

Vows ceremony. The arrangements were a "fait de complete" and Sister Vincent behaved compliantly.

Sister Zachariah arranged for the two of them to stay at a local convent. When they arrived the first night, a Superior led them to a section of the convent that had only a very large dormitory. There were at least thirty beds that resembled cots by the thickness of the mattresses. As they adjusted their eyes to the dimness of the large room, Sister Zachariah announced to Sister Vincent that they could not sleep together at night because they were guests. If they were in private rooms then sleeping together would be all right. This surprised Sister Vincent because that thought had never even entered her mind. She certainly did not want to sleep or really be with this woman whom she no longer admired nor respected.

To this day, she wonders why in the world the Mother General ever personally gave approval to Sister Vincent to be Sister Zachariah's companion on vacation. She ultimately realized that Sister Zachariah had told the Mother General that Sister Vincent had to be her companion. Sister Vincent would shortly come to find out that this same Mother General had reassigned her to an outpost of the Community in upstate New York near the Finger Lakes. Assignment to this outpost was given to those nuns who were ostensibly not following the rules and regulations of this religious community. In effect, the blame for the particular friendship that had transpired with Sister Zachariah was Sister Vincent's. The abuser, Sister Zachariah, found herself promoted to Superior and Principal of another smaller school in Parkland County.

As a result of this trip to the Long Island shore for a week, Sister Vincent lost her usual vacation on the Hudson River with all her other friends. When she returned to her home convent of four years on August 22nd, she had two days to pack her trunk with all of her possessions except what clothes would fit in her suitcase. The trunk would be shipped to St. Stanislaus' quickly. Such a bittersweet time for Sister Vincent. She had become an excellent science teacher; students in High School now came back to the elementary school to see her. She had a driver's license now. Its use for the 6-hour trip from New York City on August 30th was very helpful.

CHAPTER 15

New Scenery

S ister Vincent procured permission to drive to the Bronx to visit her mother and say goodbye until Thanksgiving. Florence did not like this change in schools. It was technically far outside the environs of the New York City archdiocese. Why now? What about Sister Zachariah? Sister Vincent's mother never liked that nun and told her daughter to stay away from her.

The morning of August 30th dawned clear and slightly chilly. There were six nuns leaving from the City at 9:00 am in a very large station wagon. They were headed North towards the Catskill Mountains, and then NNW toward their new home southeast of Syracuse and north of Binghamton in New York State. There was no banter in the car; each nun was wrapped up in her own mental conversations and memories. Sister Vincent was anxious all over again. The unknown yielded pure fear in her. She did not feel excitement as if on an adventure.

Two hours north on the Interstate highway passed quickly, or so it seemed. The next four hours were on a two-lane state highway; the ride was interminable at 45 mph with stop lights all along the way. There were hills covered with green grasses, and rolls of hay alongside yellow-orange leafed trees, while in the valleys dairy farms prevailed. Welcome to rural America, Sister Vincent - no skyscrapers, no apartment buildings, no shopping centers, only one gas station per town. This was a new world to Sister Vincent. She just wished they would arrive wherever this town of Worbuck was.

After six and a half hours, the 1965 blue Ford station wagon pulled up in front of a pretty, gabled, three-story white house with a small front porch. All six nuns, when they extricated their bodies from the car, stretched their arms out and lifted one knee after the other as if to remove the kinks from sitting in such cramped positions for so long. One by one, they walked up the three wooden steps and through the front door. The Superior, Sister Marie, was a middle-aged, tall nun from St. Louis, MO. She welcomed each one of them by their name. Sister Vincent had a hunch that this might be a much better home than the last one.

She stood in the small foyer, with the staircase to the right, and a small living room to the left. Sister Vincent followed Sister Marie up the stairs to the second floor; lo and behold, she had a large bedroom to the left of the stairway that was two times the size of the cell she had lived in for four years. There was a normal-size bed adjacent to a large window overlooking the backyard. There was a large closet, much bigger than the closets she remembered from the Bronx. Her desk was solid oak wood with three drawers on the right side. Sister Vincent sighed and smiled – so far, so good.

Sister Vincent already knew that her assignment was teaching

Science to the 7th, 8th, and 9th graders. When she asked Sister Marie where the piano lessons were held, this Superior simply stated, "Oh, we do not do that here." Have you any idea the effect of those words had on Sister Vincent's ears? Piano lessons from 3 pm until 5 pm every day after teaching from 8:30 am to 3:00 pm was the only reality she knew. Sister Marie had just added two hours to the daily routine of Sister Vincent. She was elated. Obviously, Sister Marie wanted her science teacher focused only on teaching in the classroom - more happiness for an emotionally scarred and traumatized woman.

The school was south of the house that was the convent. It was a one-story brick building with a black-topped large back yard attached to the West side of the school. There were nine classrooms, one for each grade, and a large library. The long hallway between the front door and the library was tiled half-way up the wall. The day after they arrived from New York City, Sister Marie showed Sister Vincent her Grade 8 classroom. At this school the Grade 7, 8, and 9 students changed classrooms during the day. Thus, Sister Vincent's classroom became a simplified Science Lab. Sister Marie asked Sister Vincent to make a list of chemicals she would need for demonstrations as part of the New York State science curriculum. She ordered a small amount of ether, for example, to anesthetize some fruit flies. How else could she teach about Punnett squares and genetics? She ordered some mercuric oxide to show a decomposition reaction; some iron filings and sulfur powder to illustrate a heterogenous mixture that she separated using a magnet; and a small alcohol burner with test tubes. She also listed some minerals and a smattering of each of the three types of rocks. Sister Vincent was ecstatic to have the materials she only dreamed about back in her Parkland County school.

Grade 7 students studied Life Science; Grade 8 students studied Physical Science; Grade 9 students studied Earth Science. Only now could Sister Vincent appreciate the value of Sister Martin's classes at the undergraduate college as well as the graduate Geology course she took last year. She also saw great value in current Science news. Sister Vincent collected money from each student to subscribe to the periodical "Current Science" for the year. She took 30 minutes on Friday afternoons to read the periodical with the students. It was a relaxing break for all of them. She espoused that science education and the methods of science were essential to cognitive development.

The ways of a scientist can easily be applied to everyday situations. For example, when your car engine does not start, you may suspect the battery is dead. However, a person with jumper cables attached to his car does not start your vehicle. When a tow truck arrives, the mechanic tries to turn over the engine. This knowledgeable person smiles instantaneously and declares, "M'am, you are out of gas!" This is an example of the scientific method in all its glory. First you make an observation and ask the question, why? Next a good guess (a hypothesis), then the experiment with jumper cables, followed by a new guess about the "starter" for the engine. After other observations and tests, a conclusion is made.

During December Sister Vincent felt very anxious and uneasy. During the Thanksgiving break she visited home again to finally see her family. Sister Zachariah had called and told Sister Vincent to stay with her in a convent in Manhattan. Sister Marie unwittingly gave her permission to Sister Vincent for that arrangement. Can you imagine how uncomfortable Sister Vincent felt? She barely spoke to her sponsor, Sister Zachariah. Her brother, John, picked her up every morning to spend time in the Bronx with her family.

She went to the movies with her mother on Saturday at Radio City Music Hall in Manhattan. Then they went back to the Bronx for a home-cooked meal of pork and sauerkraut and dumplings. The Worbuck station wagon left at 9 am on Sunday morning for the six-hour ride back through the rolling hills of the Finger Lakes.

At this juncture of her life, Sister Vincent was so perturbed at having seen Sister Zachariah once again, she knew she needed to take some kind of action. So, with Sister Marie's permission, she telephoned Sister Zachariah in the evening a week after Thanksgiving. Sister Vincent said only one sentence, "I never want to see you again." She repeated the sentence when Sister Zachariah asked, "What did you say?" As you may surmise, Sister Zachariah said something to the effect that she was making a grave mistake. Sister Vincent indicated that her mind was made-up. As she hung up the phone, she burst into tears. She did not know how to deal with all her emotions. They were very painful to her whole being.

By the time she knocked on Sister Marie's bedroom door she was sobbing. Sister Marie did not know how to help this young nun. She did know what had transpired. She was witness to the relationship in the Parkland County school as the other eighth grade teacher. Sister Marie had noticed how Sister Zachariah manipulated Sister Vincent. She opened a bottle of little black pills and gave one to her and told her to "sleep in" the rest of the week until breakfast. What an upheaval for Sister Vincent who had just about acclimated to her new environment. She was just starting to feel safe. Basically, she ended years of a love affair with that phone call.

In hindsight, many years later, Sister Vincent recalled that time back in 1955 when Sister Zachariah had been sent to this very same convent outpost! Could it not have been for a similar transgression all those many years ago? It was in her old age that she finally understood Sister Zachariah was a sexual predator. Sister Vincent was the victim; as such she endured years of shame and guilt. Only years of therapy helped this woman become right-minded about her relationship with Sister Zachariah. What happened between them was not Sister Vincent's fault! She was finally rid of the guilt and shame surrounding what was merely an activation of her sexual instincts. Such a rude awakening for this young woman. It could have happened in high school if perhaps she experienced more freedom and/or gained more knowledge from her mother.

CHAPTER 16

A Science Club

At some point in January, Sister Vincent asked Sister Marie if she could start a Science Club for girls. They would meet once a week after school. Of course, the answer from Sister Marie was, "Yes." She admired the initiative of her young science teacher. The purpose of the club was to use the scientific method to answer questions outside the regular course of study. One of the questions that arose during the early Spring was, "What do the internal organs of a mammal really look like?" Ah, Sister Vincent supplied the answer to that question.

There were four small white mice residents of the 8th Grade Science room. There was still some ether left over from the fruit fly experiments the group completed in the Fall. If they anesthetized the mouse, Sister Vincent could use a new dissecting instrument to carefully open the underbelly of the mouse with a vertical incision. Then, the girls could see for themselves the internal organs: the beating heart, the stomach, the liver, the intestines, and the lungs as miniature as they were. A discussion ensued about the mouse waking up from the ether. What were they going to do with this tiny animal that was still alive?

One girl suggested sewing up the skin of the mouse very carefully. The others agreed in unison and begged Sister Vincent to let them do this. She went over to the house to get them a needle and white thread. When she returned to the classroom, Sister lit a match to sterilize the needle's tip after Nancy, the President of the Club, threaded the needle. Nancy gave the needle to Penny who gingerly sewed the mouse's skin back together again without pricking a single internal organ. Voila, Sister Vincent put the mouse back in its house and left him overnight to recuperate. Sister said some prayers that the little white mammal would be alive in the morning.

Why, yes indeed, the mouse was up and started eating when Sister Vincent turned the lights on in her classroom. Sister Marie was with her because she had concern if the animal had died how these young girls would deal with the unfortunate trauma. Glee abounded that morning – a couple of girls thought it was a miracle. Each of the classes that day heard the compelling story of the *school mouse*. What Sister Vincent did not know about Penny was that her father was a writer for the local newspaper. Penny said her father was stopping by after school to see the mouse. Well, a story was written and there was a picture of Sister Vincent and Penny holding the mouse in the morning edition of the following day's newspaper. She sent a copy of the article home to the Bronx; her mother saved it during all her years alive. After her death, it was returned to Sister Vincent by her brother. It became such a sweet memory for her to have.

During the Spring break in 1968, Sister Marie asked Sister Vincent to invite her mother to come and spend the week with them. So, the same station wagon that carried seven nuns south to New York City became a taxi for her mother to have a week's vacation from her job in mid-town Manhattan. A friend of Sister Marie's was the north-bound driver of this station wagon. Once again, Sister Vincent did not know what to expect from this unorthodox visit. Her relationship with her mother was a tenuous one. Florence obviously loved her daughter; subconsciously Sister Vincent harbored all sorts of resentments against her mother. After graduating from high school, she had never learned how to have an adult conversation with her mother. In addition, there had been Sister Zachariah who became a surrogate mother to this deprived child. Pauline endured years of criticism from both her parents. Nor was there any show of affection or praise from Florence or Vincent.

With that backdrop, the first two days went well in spite of Sister Vincent's feeling uncomfortable. Mid-week Sister Marie's friend drove the three of them to Syracuse. Two-by-two they walked to a movie theater showing, "Guess Who's Coming to Dinner?". How unusual was that in the late 60s? Was it not the, "Age of Aquarius"? Freedom demonstrations were the norm for that time in history. Familiar with world news, Sister Marie was happily at the forefront of religious acceptance of changes in their code of behavior. As an example, the stiff black veil they wore for decades changed into a soft black veil minus the stiff white covering around their face and ears.

When Friday rolled around, Sister Marie wanted Sister Vincent to be a driver of the station wagon headed back to New York City. Early that morning, during Mass, Sister Vincent felt nauseous.

Anxiety enveloped her again. Yes, it had something to do with being in such close proximity to her mother for six days. Sister Vincent was acutely aware that she could not drive to the City. Sister Marie seemed disappointed in her decision. Sister Vincent told the three of them she had a stomach bug and needed to stay home. In all probability, Sister Marie, the Superior terribly missed *her* mother living in St. Louis, MO. Permission to see her mother once a year was never granted. Sister Marie assumed that Sister Vincent would be thrilled to be with her mother for a week. However, she saw no evidence of any affection between the two.

Sometime in April of 1968 Sister Marie met with the Worbuck High School Principal, Mr. Thompson. The purpose of the visit involved the curriculum and studies of the Grade 9 students in her Catholic (parochial) school. Sister Marie felt proud to inform this gentleman that her 9th Grade class would be able to follow the exact same Earth Science curriculum as his public-school students next year. This was an accomplishment to have these 9th grade graduates move right into the public high school's sequence of science subjects. The students would also receive free textbooks from the high school. Sister Marie left with a copy of the new text: the ESCP - Earth Science Curriculum Project book. When she showed the textbook to Sister Vincent, the young nun responded with enthusiasm. Earth Science was a subject she really liked and enjoyed teaching. Her course background included Astronomy, Geology and Oceanography. She was more than qualified to teach this new course.

Since the school and convent were closed during July and August, Sister Marie received a letter from the Mother General of the Congregation during the first week of June. The document contained the nuns' assignments for the next academic year. Sister Marie opened this letter as they finished supper in the refectory (the small dining room). As she looked at the list, she took off her glasses, she laid them on top of the letter, and she looked out the window to her right. She was not smiling. The other six nuns watched Sister Marie intently; she seemed perturbed. She sighed as she told them that everybody was returning to Worbuck *except* Sister Vincent! Sister Marie said to her science teacher, "You are assigned to the Motherhouse to teach at the new Rosary Academy. I am very disappointed because of the arrangements I made with Mr. Thompson for you to teach the ninth graders the new Earth Science curriculum."

Sister Vincent was visibly disappointed. She liked Worbuck as well as Sister Marie and her own creation - the Science room. Sister Vincent was also genuinely excited about the new ESCP course of study just instituted. On the other hand, she was *not* at all thrilled to be returning to the Motherhouse under the scrutinizing eyes of many Superiors. The facts were: it was a brand-new high school; secondly, it was comparable to a promotion for her - going from the junior high school grades to a high school position. Neither of those facts enthused Sister Vincent. She still responded to change with anxiety and fear.

Science curricula were exploding. It was their heyday. There was money to be had from the NSF to train teachers in the ways of science education. There was money for science materials as well as equipment. Science was certainly not just information and facts. It was learning to think and perform in the way that research scientists think and perform experiments. Luckily for Sister Vincent she inherited from her grandfather a love of the natural world. Harry Wold was the editor-in-chief of the Chemical Engineering News. He taught her about atoms when she was five years old. Sister Vincent possessed an astute logical brain. She used it well throughout her life while teaching.

Sister Vincent needed to pack her trunk with her meager nunnery possessions. The more difficult task was to disassemble the Science room with its posters, safety signs, jugs of water, buckets, beakers and chemicals. All of these things belonged under lock and key. Who knew if this classroom would ever again be a "Science Lab"?

The young adolescents in the Science Club were visibly upset to learn that Sister Vincent was not returning next year. There was a definite mutual respect between the girls and Sister Vincent. School for them had become fun! Sister Vincent liked the girls and she also had fun when she was working with them.

The last day of school was a half-day. Sister Marie planned a small party for her teachers at the noontime dinner. It was a relaxing event with lots of laughter. Once again, Sister Vincent felt isolated and alone. She was on the verge of tears as she said good-bye to her colleagues, her new friends in this bucolic home. Sister Vincent drove the station wagon with three other nuns to Parkland County the next morning.

When she arrived, Sister Vincent reported to a different elderly Superior – a governess for all professed and working nuns residing at the Motherhouse. This nun had a furrowed brow, a frozen stare, and thin lips that were straight across without the slightest curve to them. This Superior gave Sister Vincent her room number in a new wing of the Motherhouse. Her daily charge or job was to clean the bathrooms in the new wing.

Sister Vincent picked up both her suitcase and black leather book bag; she left the office in search of her new living quarters. The new wing was across the swamp towards the college. It was a long rectangular building with cells on both sides of the hallway. All the professed nuns working anywhere on this campus lived there. Her cell was essentially the same as other cells in all convents except for Worbuck, New York.

It was June 1968. If the truth be told, Sister Vincent had not yet quite recovered from the sexual episode with Sister Zachariah. A startling thing had happened to her a month later, back in 1967, while trying to fall asleep. She was lying on her stomach and discovered that she could easily rub her pubic area on the mattress. Sister Vincent experienced the same sense of pleasurable relief while doing this. She did not know the word, "masturbation", nor anything about it. She never spoke to another living soul about this activity.

Sister Vincent did not engage in masturbation while living in upstate New York. It just did not happen. However, now situated in her new living quarters, it seemed to be the norm for her most nights. Whether it was right or wrong did not matter to her. Sister Vincent seemed to have no control over it happening. She continued her summer assignment as the Chemistry Lab instructor for the third year. This job entailed precisely preparing solutions as well as cleaning equipment and getting materials ready for the next Lab session.

CHAPTER 17

A Decision

Sometime after the 4th of July holiday and celebration in 1968, Sister Vincent said to herself one night after she discovered how to pleasure herself, "There has to be more to life than this solitary existence." At that moment in time she decided to leave the convent. Her mind was made up – she had had enough of this way of life; she had no voice in decisions to remain in a particular parish school. Her life existed at the whim of the Mother General and her associates. In her heart she was rebelling against the three vows of poverty, chastity, and obedience.

In June of 1967, her brother John, about to be ordained a deacon, decided that celibacy and the priesthood were *not* for him. He left the Seminary; he encountered his mother's anger and embarrassment that her son would not be a priest. John proceeded to introduce the family to the love of his life, Elizabeth. They had met each other during the summer of 1966 at the New Jersey shore. Sister Vincent liked Elizabeth. She was open and honest; she herself had spent a short time in a convent. Their wedding day occurred on the last Saturday of July in 1968.

The day of John and Betty's wedding dawned warm, clear and sunny. Sister Vincent had permission to spend the weekend in the Bronx staying at the local parish convent. She chose a good friend of hers, an alumnus of the same high school, to be her companion. Her friend, Mary, was also now a professed nun. Together they attended the ceremony in the morning witnessing John and Elizabeth's exchange of vows. Sister Vincent noticed how all of the newlywed's friends were smiling and laughing. Essentially, those friends were a very happy group of young people.

The reception was crowded with relatives and friends of Sister Vincent's family on one side; all Elizabeth's relatives and friends sat on the opposite side of the banquet hall. What she remembers most about that reception was one of her first cousins getting her drunk. He kept getting her a refill of Seagram's and 7-Up. Her friend, Sister Mary had to guide her out of the hall as the celebration ended. Please remember that Sister Vincent's decision to come home and live with her mother and brothers again in their four-room apartment was a done deal. She chose not to impose on John's day and tell anyone, save Sister Mary, that she would no longer be a nun in two weeks.

You see, shortly after that 4th of July holiday and her momentous decision, Sister Vincent made an appointment to see the same Mother General who had witnessed her first vows and then her final vows. Because the vows of chastity, obedience and poverty she uttered for the 'rest of her life' in 1967, Sister Vincent needed permission from Rome to be relieved of her vows. She told the

Mother General that fateful morning about her decision to leave the Community.

Quite unfortunately, the Mother General told Sister Vincent that she could *not* leave. She needed her for the Science position at the new high school across the state highway from the Motherhouse. Sister Vincent said again, "I am leaving." Well then, the Mother General said, "You must go over to the high school and inform the Principal that you will not be there next month." "Fine, I will," said Sister Vincent as she left the office. Sister Vincent went directly across the road to see the Principal in this new building. This middle-aged nun was at least sympathetic and wished her well.

During the second week of July, the Mother General called for Sister Vincent. This supreme head of the Community told her that she had made an appointment for Sister Vincent to see the Monsignor in charge of the Chancery in Manhattan. The Chancery, an extension of St. Patrick's Cathedral, was the residence of the Cardinal of the Archdiocese of New York. Monsignor Flannery was the Cardinal's personal assistant. Sister Vincent walked into Monsignor's office enveloped by a huge mahogany desk with thick brocade drapes behind the desk covering the window. It was a relatively small room for such a large desk. There was no natural light in this office only the scattered glow from overhead fluorescent bulbs.

He was a middle-aged priest, grey hair at his temples, dressed in a black suit with a white collar around his neck. His red beret was off to the side of the desk on a small table. He smiled at Sister Vincent in an effort to seem friendly. He asked her why she wanted to leave the convent after taking final vows? Sister Vincent was not prepared for this question. Her heart was pounding, her hands were sweaty as she faced yet another hurdle to escape the austerity of convent life. She simply stated that she thought there was more to life. She had to find out if this was true.

The Monsignor mentioned the dispensation from Rome that she needed. Sister Vincent just shook her head in abeyance and uttered, "I know." Then Monsignor Flannery strongly urged her to seek counseling. He was positive that this would help her with her decision. He would make all the arrangements for her. Sister Vincent was thinking, uh-oh, there must be something wrong with me. What was this counseling all about, anyway? The 1960s were just the beginning of therapeutic counseling before the turn of the Century when almost everybody was in therapy. She slowly thanked the Monsignor and declined his invitation for counseling. "I am leaving", were her parting words. In hindsight many years later, she realized that the Mother General no doubt told him about the sexual relationship that had occurred.

The next hurdle was to talk to her mother. She feared her wrath. One week after John's wedding, the first weekend in August, she drove to the Bronx on a very warm and humid Saturday. She arrived at the apartment unannounced; her mother was busy packing a suitcase for a two-week vacation. Florence was travelling with a friend to a rental cottage on the New Jersey shore near a beach and the ocean. Sister Vincent finally spoke up and said, "Mom, I am leaving the convent and coming home."

"Oh NO, why are you doing that? What are going to do with yourself? What will my friends and neighbors say? First John comes home and now you! Well, I will tell you one thing, I am not giving up my vacation and staying home just for you. You are on your own."

Sister Vincent replied, "I will find a job teaching Science. I have experience; I have my College degree; and I have New York State certification. I just can't stay there any longer. There has to be more to life."

Sister Vincent asked her mother for clothes to wear next week when she left the convent. Her mother went to her stuffed narrow closet and from the very back end she pulled out a matching pink floral skirt and top. The clothes fit Sister Vincent, but the skirt was certainly too long for 1968 fashion. She would need help shortening the skirt. Her mother also gave her a pair of beige pantyhose to wear with her black nun's shoes. The last thing Florence told her was to go to a department store on 5th Avenue and get her hair fixed on the day she left. She should charge the cost of the hair cut to her mother's account. And so, she left her mother without a hug or a kiss from her. She drove herself back to the Motherhouse. Florence was beside herself with confusion and utter disappointment.

With everything finalized, Sister Vincent told two or three of the nuns living near her in the long hallway that she was leaving to go home in a few days. She listened to their well wishes. They laughed about the clothes her mother had given her. How *old* were they? One of the Sisters, a needle and thread expert, shortened the pink skirt for her. Another Sister asked if she could trim her hair? Sister Vincent declined. What in the world would Sister Vincent look like when she changed out of her habit, black veil and into these "street clothes"?

Sister Vincent next needed to pack her trunk to send it home to the Bronx. Religious items she gave away to those nuns that were helping her. She packed a pile of school notebooks and their syllabi from every single college class. She still had all of her sheet music, plus additional music for the hymns that she used with children's choirs. She had copies of all the lesson plans from her six years of teaching. The trunk was ready to go at the end of that weekend. One major task accomplished.

Sister Vincent still had the same black suitcase that she used on Entrance Day as a postulant. She could pack her underwear and robe and clothes from her mother to take to East 62nd Street. The building, an old brownstone, was the first convent building of the Community in the late 1800s. For some odd reason in 1968 this place was where nuns who were leaving were released. So, on August 5th, her Dad's birthday, a senior nun drove Sister Vincent into Manhattan and just dropped her off in front of the convent brownstone. She climbed the steep stone staircase and rang the bell.

The parlor, on the right of the vestibule, was no bigger than 8 feet by 8 feet. Sister Vincent was told to sit there; within five minutes two nuns came into the very small room with ginger ale and cookies. Sister Vincent had no interest in either. The older of the two nuns asked, "Who is coming to get you?" Sister Vincent replied, "No one is coming to get me. I'm leaving on my own."

A discussion ensued about the logistics of leaving. What was she going to do? Why was no one coming? How would she get home? Sister Vincent could not believe she had to sit there and listen to all these questions and answer them. "I will get on the subway and go home to the Bronx. I have a key to my mother's apartment", is all she would say.

Sister Vincent finally asked, "Where do I get changed?" They pointed to a small guest lavatory across the hallway where she changed out of her habit and veil. Quickly she dressed in the pink floral skirt and top and re-entered the parlor. The younger of the two nuns handed her a check for $200.00, the return of her dowry. Sister Vincent thanked the Sisters and finally took her first step out into New York City; she took a deep breath and descended the stairs. Each step represented the courage it took to start life all over again. Pauline was *free* and glad of it. There was no anxiety or fear this time as she made her way west towards 5th Avenue.

CHAPTER 18

A New World

Pauline's first task was to find a bank to cash the $200. check. She needed some money for both lunch and the subway ride home. She walked into a large 5th Avenue bank and presented the check to the teller.

"Do you have an account with us?"

"No, I do not. I just left a Convent, and this is what they gave me. I have no cash. I need money to get home."

"Let me see your driver's license, please."

Pauline presented a New York State license issued to Sister Vincent, Worbuck, NY. The teller took the check and license over to a supervisor behind a desk. Returning to the counter, she slid the check and the license back to Pauline.

"I'm sorry we cannot cash this check. If you go down to 47th Street, the bank there that issued this check may be able to help you."

Now, this provoked some anxiety and a little anger. Why would the Community give her a check if she could not cash it? Her vow of poverty prevented her from having a bank account. She continued walking South on Fifth Avenue. She had memorized the name of the bank and found it on the East side of the street. Pauline was on the West side. At the corner of 47th Street she waited for the green light, walked across the street directly into the bank that held the religious community's money. She knew the routine and presented the check and her driver's license to the teller.

"I have just left this convent and they gave me this check. I have no money to get home."

The teller took the check and her license behind a closed door. The teller emerged and smiled as she said, "This will take a little time. Mr. Cheuy must call the signaturee of the check by phone to verify this check is not stolen."

Pauline's face became flushed as if she were guilty of wrongdoing. You see, she had left the confines of the convent without any practice in dealing and speaking confidently with other adults. The irony was that she was an excellent communicator with teenagers in a classroom. This disparity lasted for five or six more years to her professional detriment.

After 30 minutes waiting in a chair near the lobby, a gentleman approached her and called her by name,

"Pauline, come with me. I will be happy to cash this check for you today. In the future, you will need an account in this bank for me to authorize cashing a check for this amount."

Pauline signed the check, "Sister Vincent Hurtt". The teller wrote her license number under her signature and proceeded to count out ten $20 bills. Her anxiety started to subside as she left the bank with her own money. This was the first time in eight years she had real money to spend. She decided to go into a Horn and Hardart's and get something to eat for the cost of 50 cents. It was a self-serve cafeteria with vertical rows of small windows on the wall to the left. Each little window showed the food at that location. You simply inserted your dimes and nickels; the little door opened for you to retrieve your sandwich or soup or cookies. She felt safe here; it was a favorite stop when visiting the city as a child with her grandmother or her aunt.

So began the start of Pauline's new life. She did not know where it would lead. She never questioned her decision to leave the convent even once. She began to make her own choices. Years later, as the elder of her family of origin, she would tell them that the path was not at all an easy one. However, she did not regret anything that she lived through for the ensuing 50 years. Life is, oh, so happy and blessed for anyone who heals their broken heart.

CHAPTER 19

Year 2020

*I*n the year of 2020, this story of apparent ignorance may seem trivial and/or implausible. However, the lifestyle of the 1950s was a segregated one. There were no support groups; there were no senior centers; there were no parent advisory boards. Most people knew a few of their neighbors in a single apartment building. That was the extent of their socialization.

As a new mother, Florence in this story, did not know what to do with Pauline on several occasions. A quick knock on a neighbor's door yielded a woman who would tell her what to do with this child. There were no parenting groups or gatherings. In the late 1940s, Dr. Spock published a book about babies and children. It became a bible to parents with kids.

In most cases, in the 1950s, families were a tight knit group. They lived near each other; they always celebrated together; they visited each other every week; they watched the new babies grow to be toddlers and then young children; they talked to their adult siblings at least once a week on a wired phone on a desk or a wall.

Now in 2020, families are scattered. Parents and siblings do not live near each other; the children may not know their grandparents or cousins; they celebrate occasionally; they communicate non-verbally with a text message or an email.

According to 2020 standards, if two nuns in a convent mutually desire to sleep together, for comfort, for warm feelings of sentimentality, for the touch of another human being, why is that a problem? The problem occurs when there is a lack of equality in the relationship. This lack of equality is tantamount to abuse.

The Catholic Church has been ravaged by the onslaught of sexual abuse allegations against priests. It was unfortunately a commonplace occurrence. What about religious women? There are few "nun" allegations. Yet, an older nun once asked my friend, a newly professed nun, "Will you be my 'puff'?" Translated, take care of me and sleep with me. The age difference was great enough to have the power in the hands of the older woman.

What about the pastors who get attracted to nuns? The power, here, resides with the priest. The nuns in this case suffer sexual abuse at the hands of the cleric.

What priests and/or ministers have allegedly done to young boys and seminarians is merely the tip of the iceberg for Christian Churches. Because celibacy is *not* natural, historically slaves and orphans have been objects of sexual encounters. What a Church never speaks about is that one or two of the Apostles had wives.

Just as religion is *not* spirituality. Churches are groups of like-minded individuals connected to one another through their faith. Connections are the way toward the betterment of our world. Such groups are a blessing! May we all be connected to one another serving our communities.

"Let peace fill our hearts and our homes until it overflows into our world." (Anonymous)

EPILOGUE

*H*aving survived the abusive experience with Sister Zachariah, Pauline went on to teach Physical Science to Grade 9 students, and ultimately served her employers as a renowned Chemistry teacher of 10th and 11th grade students. Of particular note, is that she was chosen as the Chemistry teacher for the Massachusetts Academy of Math and Science. Her career also included In-service presentations to other teachers for CEUs. She loved teaching and retired after 45 years only because of osteoarthritic knees that prevented her from standing and walking.

It is worthy of note that the lingering effects of the convent emotional and sexual abuse ultimately impinged on Pauline's ability to establish and maintain meaningful and healthy relationships. When she left the convent, there was a desire to explore heterosexual possibilities. These relationships were absent from her life before the convent. There was some trial and error during her first summer on the New Jersey shore. Her first experience with intercourse was lackluster. She did discover that she could be attractive to the opposite sex.

Two years later Pauline became involved in a summer romance

that lasted one year. After this, she found herself attracted to a recluse. She tried helping him and they were married without much fanfare. It only lasted two years. Pauline became the victim of physical abuse without any sex in this relationship. She discovered the man was a bisexual. She filed for a divorce. She felt like a failure.

Her first attempt at psychotherapy was with a psychiatric MD that resulted in another unfortunate violation of her person. He actually showed up at her apartment one day unannounced to have sex with her. How was she ever going to learn to trust another person – male or female? This therapeutic relationship continued until one day on the phone, she repeated the words, "I never want to see you again." Those were the exact words she had said to Sister Zachariah. It was the only way she knew how to deal with another abusive relationship.

Enter suitor #2. Sam was educated. He had a compulsive personality. A long-distance romance developed between September and January. He moved and then resided with Pauline. A healthy sexual relationship was not part of this partnership either. She willingly married him after a tragic accident that left him a paraplegic in a wheelchair. After 6 years of being a caregiver with none of her needs met, she filed for divorce #2. This represented yet another failure for Pauline.

During this time, she drove 35 minutes to her school teaching job. One Monday morning she was completely overwhelmed with a sinking feeling of dread and panic that froze her to the steering wheel as she parked her car. She had no clue what was happening to her. She gradually got herself together and went through her day teaching six classes. She felt nauseous and anxious when she got home that day. Her only recourse was alcohol. It calmed her down. She became a daily drinker to relieve the pervasive anxiety that she constantly felt.

The following morning the identical feelings of dread, fear, and anxiety gripped her again with more intensity. She was crying. She was early to school and able to make a phone call to her sister-in-law. Her brother was able to track down a PhD psychotherapist who would see her. Her first appointment with this younger male yielded an evening appointment with an MD psychiatrist as a medication referral. He listened to her symptoms and prescribed an anti-depressant and an anti-anxiety medication. He further explained that her father also probably resorted to alcohol to relieve his feelings of depression and/or anxiety.

Her therapy with this same young psychotherapist continued satisfactorily for twenty plus years. She learned:

- she was a victim of PTSD,
- she was an Adult Child of an Alcoholic,
- she was an addict to alcohol and food.
- she was clinically depressed

Her homosexual relationship in the convent was not her fault. The guilt and shame she carried unconsciously came to light as she talked to this man twice a week for several years. Pauline learned when shame takes root, it can harm self-image; it can lead to disconnection from others; it can contribute to deeper mental health issues such as depression and substance abuse.

Abandonment issues derived from both her mother and Sister

Zachariah fueled her gargantuan fear of being alone. When a storm was approaching, she operated in a panic mode. Pauline basically *never* felt safe.

In desperation and the hopeless state of mind that persisted Pauline attended an Alcoholics Anonymous meeting in her hometown on the Sunday of Labor Day weekend in 1986. Her attendance at Adult Children of Alcoholics meetings every week for two prior years had given her an insight to her own drinking problem.

So it was, in 1986, Pauline became sober (stopped drinking altogether). She interacted well with the men and women in her AA "home" group. She felt comfortable among other alcoholics. She became stable enough to change jobs and further her career. Because she had moved to a new town, her old therapist was an hour's drive away. Her visits to him became maintenance sessions once a month. No one else knew her as well as he did. Pauline's feelings of fear and anxiety still occasionally overwhelmed her.

Enter suitor #3. Joe was a sober alcoholic. He was intelligent and friendly, but hesitant to have sex with her. Once again, Pauline settled for less than she deserved. They were predictably married. It was not a happy marriage by any means. He was impotent; he took advantage of her good will; he never contributed to the overhead of the condominium she owned; he had a blue-collar job. Joe could have had a better job with his education degree and his ability to read, write, and speak Chinese.

After three years of dealing with his addiction to hard-core pornography, Pauline politely asked him to leave her home. Joe resumed drinking alcohol every day. She then told him emphatically to leave. He was egotistical and refused to leave. At this time, overeating became a habit for Pauline. Her weight ballooned close to 300 pounds.

Joe's severe cold turned into an ambulance ride to the nearest hospital and an ICU admittance one day in January 2010. After a week he was diagnosed with idiopathic interstitial lung disease that led to pulmonary fibrosis. He was on oxygen for the final two years of his life. His drinking and smoking continued. Pauline became a caretaker again as was her pattern. The anger sizzled and became bottled up inside of her for years.

After two years in and out of Nursing Homes, he died of his lung disease. He was totally incapacitated at the time of his death. After his death and cremation, Pauline was once again free. Had she finally learned *her* life lesson?

The answer was yes and no. Yes, she made decisions without need for approval again. Just as she executed her decision to leave the religious community, she re-located to a retirement community in the South, against the advice of family and friends.

Her addiction to alcohol progressed to the point of almost killing her. She was drinking more than four liters of wine every day – one glass after the other. Pauline would drink until she blacked out. One morning she woke up on the floor of a room where she did not drink. She had no recollection of how she got there.

The following day, Pauline knew she had to return to Alcoholics Anonymous or die! She returned to AA and at this writing she is six years sober. Pauline has a group of AA friends she considers her family. They are a tight knit group of friends. They have her back.

She can ask for help for any need that she has. Pauline is happy and content for the first time in her life. She relishes each morning when she wakes up to another day of freedom and happiness.

Yes, Pauline has finally learned *her* life lesson!

Printed in Poland
by Amazon Fulfillment
Poland Sp. z o.o., Wrocław

60550575R00073